Information Management

U.S. Marine Corps

PCN 143 000094 00

DISTRIBUTION STATEMENT A: Approved for public; distribution is unlimited

To Our Readers

Changes: Readers of this publication are encouraged to submit suggestions and changes that will improve it. Recommendations may be sent directly to Commanding General, Marine Corps Combat Development Command, Doctrine Division (C 42), 3300 Russell Road, Suite 318A, Quantico, VA 22134-5021 or by fax to 703-784-2917 (DSN 278-2917) or by E-mail to **morgann@mccdc.usmc.mil**. Recommendations should include the following information:

- Location of change
    - Publication number and title
    - Current page number
    - Paragraph number (if applicable)
    - Line number
    - Figure or table number (if applicable)
- Nature of change
    - Add, delete
    - Proposed new text, preferably double-spaced and typewritten
- Justification and/or source of change

Additional copies: A printed copy of this publication may be obtained from Marine Corps Logistics Base, Albany, GA 31704-5001, by following the instructions in MCBul 5600, *Marine Corps Doctrinal Publications Status*. An electronic copy may be obtained from the Doctrine Division, MCCDC, world wide web home page which is found at the following universal reference locator: **http://www.doctrine.usmc.mil**.

**Unless otherwise stated, whenever the masculine gender is used, both
men and women are included.**

DEPARTMENT OF THE NAVY
Headquarters United States Marine Corps
Washington, D.C. 20308-1775

24 January 2002

FOREWORD

Marine Corps Warfighting Publication (MCWP) 3-40.2, *Information Management*, builds on the doctrinal foundation established by Marine Corps Doctrinal Publication 6, *Command and Control*. As set forth in MCDP 6, information management is one of the three basic elements of command and control (C2), the other two elements are people and C2 support. MCWP 3-40.2 explains how information supports the C2 process and how it assists those who plan, decide, execute, and assess. It presents all users and handlers of information with a variety of techniques and guidelines to manage information effectively in order to support the assessment and decisionmaking processes. Specifically, MCWP 3-40.2 discusses the fundamentals of information, personnel responsibilities, C2 support structure development, and security of information.

Reviewed and approved this date.

BY DIRECTION OF THE COMMANDANT OF THE MARINE CORPS

EDWARD HANLON, JR.
Lieutenant General, U.S. Marine Corps
Commanding General
Marine Corps Combat Development Command

DISTRIBUTION: 143 000094 00

INFORMATION MANAGEMENT

TABLE OF CONTENTS

Chapter 3   Command and Control Support Structure Development

Chapter 4   Security

Appendices

Notes

Glossary

References and Related Publications

CHAPTER 1
FUNDAMENTALS OF INFORMATION

The term information generically refers to all facts, data, or instructions in any medium or form. The commander requires quality information to understand situations and events and to quickly control the challenges that confront him. Marine Corps Doctrinal Publication (MCDP) 6, *Command and Control*, states that information serves two purposes: to help create situational awareness as the basis for decisions and to direct and coordinate actions in the execution of a decision. Quality information adds value to the decisionmaking process and is critical to the success or failure of an operation. Therefore, the commander must determine his information requirements and ensure that information is managed effectively.

The Marine Corps operating environment of today and the emerging threats of tomorrow require force mobility, unit dispersion, and command agility. As we move into the 21st century, the ability to simultaneously share quality information from various locations will be necessary if the commander is to make effective command and control (C2) decisions. Information management addresses information as a commodity instead of a technology and is performed at all levels, regardless of the extent of automation. Effective information management delivers critically important information in a timely manner to those who need it in a form that they can quickly understand.

Information management includes all activities involved in the identification, collection, filtering, fusing, processing, focusing, dissemination, and usage of information. It assembles information that promotes understanding of the battlespace and enables the commander to better formulate and analyze courses of action, make decisions, execute those decisions, and understand results from previous decisions. Information management provides the quality information a commander needs to support the decisionmaking

process. The role of information management is to provide a timely flow of relevant information that enables the commander to anticipate changing conditions and understand its impact on current and future operations.

Information and the Commander

The commander makes decisions based on his understanding of the location, disposition, and status of friendly and enemy forces. Historically, a commander achieved situational awareness by personally viewing the battle. As the size and scope of competing forces and the battlespace increased, the commander's ability to fully understand the battle became limited. To achieve understanding, a commander began to use situation maps, textual material (e.g., messages, reports, status boards), and voice reports in conjunction with his experience (i.e., intuitive reasoning and judgment) and personal contact with frontline units to make decisions. However, information that provided enhanced understanding of the situation or event was often available, but it was not provided to the commander in a timely manner or in a form that they could quickly understand.

Today, the commander's and the staff's information requirements remain relatively the same—they still rely on quality information to attain an understanding of the battlespace. What has changed is the technological capability to produce and disseminate enormous amounts of data. The role of information management is to provide a timely flow of relevant information that supports all aspects of the planning, decision, execution, and assessment (PDE&A) cycles of numerous, and potentially widely dispersed, units. Automated capabilities and commonly understood procedures are used to display battlespace information in a dynamic environment and to rapidly gain understanding in order to make effective decisions.

The philosophy contained in MCDP 6 emphasizes that Marines must learn to operate in an environment of uncertainty, and that combat is by its very nature chaotic, disruptive, and unpredictable. Information collected in such an environment can often be inaccurate or misleading, and it may be not be important, relevant, or available within the time constraints of the commander's decisionmaking process. Technological advances have further placed enormous amounts of information at a commander's fingertips: more information is available than one Marine can possibly collate, assimilate, and evaluate.

Simply collecting and disseminating volumes of information does not reduce information overload. Information management offers a solution to the information requirements of decisionmaking. Effective information management procedures enable users to reap the benefits of technology while providing quality information to commanders thereby facilitating decisionmaking, strengthening command and control, and avoiding information overload.

MCDP 6 states that the three elements of command and control are information, people, and C2 support structure (see fig. 1-1), and that they must interact seamlessly to produce effective and harmonious actions. These three elements provide the commander with the tools needed to develop and execute effective information management procedures that support all aspects of decisionmaking.

Principles

The following principles are required to efficiently and effectively manage information and should guide the information management program at every level of command in order to facilitate decisionmaking. These principles apply to every situation that requires a decision.

Use Requirements to Define the Information Flow

Command relationships, organization of the force, and information needs influence the flow of information. Recognition of user requirements and the resulting information flow allows commands to apply the proper mix of personnel, equipment, training, procedures, and network infrastructure to produce the information needed to make decisions.

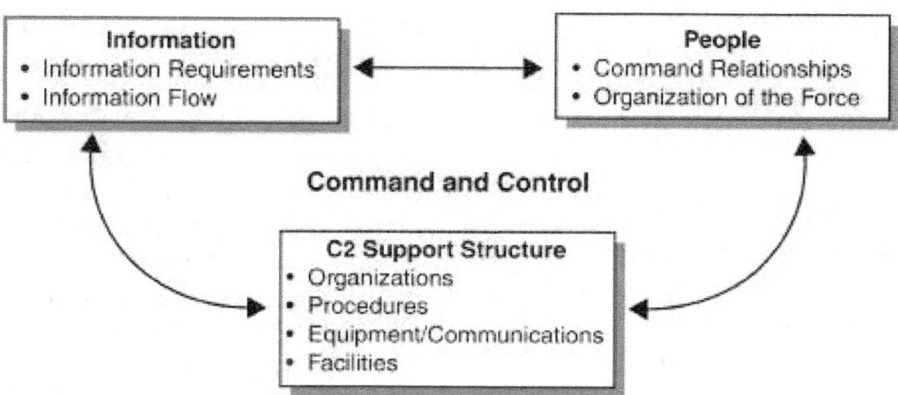

Figure 1-1. Elements of Command and Control.

Tailor Information for the Commander

Filter out unnecessary, redundant, or irrelevant information according to the defined information requirements in order to prevent information overload. Provide information in the format specified by the commander.

Use Multiple Sources of Information

Knowledge is normally gained from information derived from numerous products that have been fused together. The use of multiple sources normally improves information accuracy and reduces error. But it can also increases network traffic and add to the delay between gathering information and gaining knowledge. Therefore, there needs to be a balance between collecting, processing, and dissemination.

Deliver Information on Time

The delivery of information in a timely manner is critical. When requesting information, the requestor should clearly state when the information is required. The information should then be delivered to the requestor in a timely manner. Information that is late does not support the decisionmaking process.

Disseminate Accurate and Relevant Information

Inaccurate or irrelevant information is worse than no information at all. However, even fragmentary information that supports critical information requirements may be of some value if it is validated and provided in a timely manner in a form that is clearly understood.

Create Flexible and Redundant Procedures and Plans

The information management plan must be able to overcome changes generated by battle damage, sudden increases in the volume of information, and the needs of different commanders at all echelons of command. The information management plan should have redundant capabilities and incorporate back up procedures, alternate paths, and primary and alternate personnel/organizations. It should avoid having any "single point of failure" anywhere in the network, security, information, or information assurance architectures.

Protect Information Through a Vigorous Security Program

Information management must assure the integrity of the information and the sources/databases from which that information was derived. Corrupted or degraded information is of little value and adversely affects the quality of the decisionmaking process.

Classes of Information Within an Information Hierarchy

There are four classes of information within the information hierarchy: raw data, processed data (information), knowledge, and understanding. Each class of information has its own distinct role in the decisionmaking process. The graduations between the different classes may not always be clear, but as information moves through the information hierarchy (see fig. 1-2 on page 1-4), it becomes more valuable to the decisionmaker. Information management's goal is to facilitate the development of quality information throughout the information hierarchy, thus increasing its value and relevance and ensuring the development of understanding by the commander.

Some level of situational awareness can be achieved with raw data, but situational awareness tends to strengthen as information moves through the information hierarchy. Enhanced situational awareness enables the commander to be better prepared to anticipate future conditions, visualize operations, provide guidance, and accurately assess situations. Developing accurate situational awareness with limited and uncertain

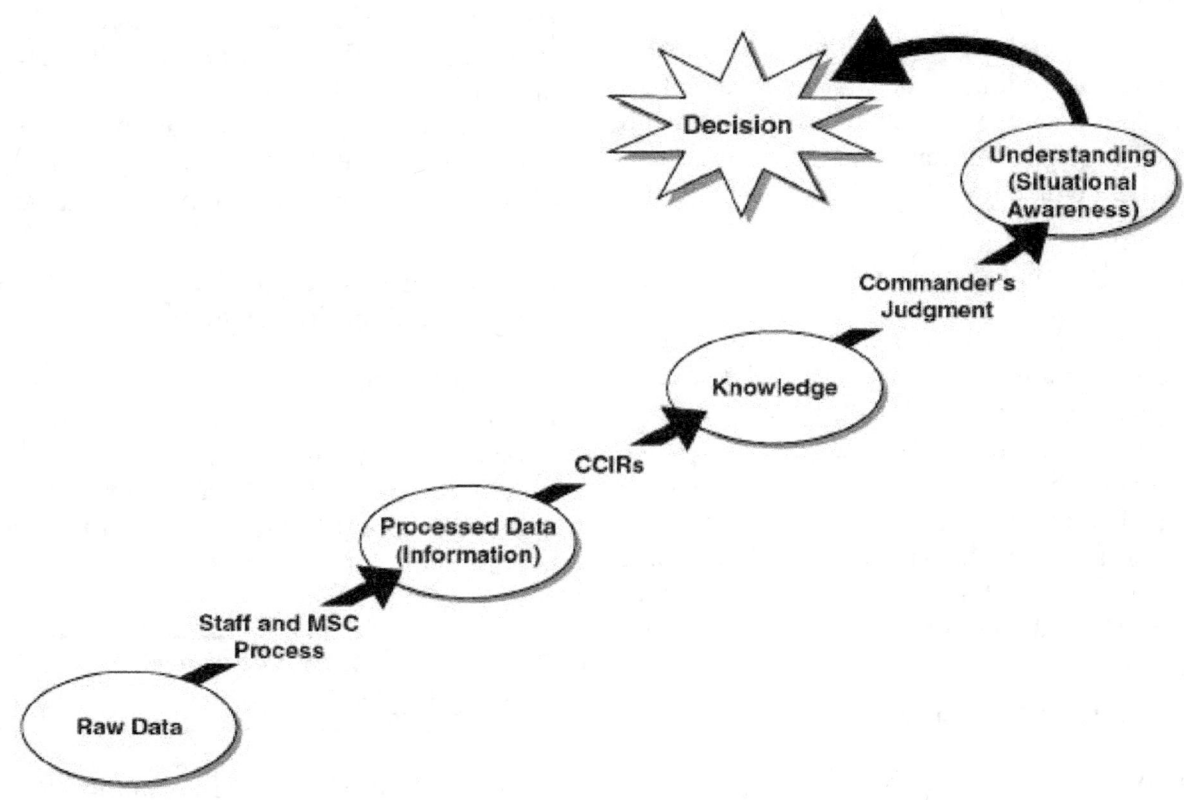

Figure 1-2. Information Flow Through the Information Hierarchy.

information under severe time constraints is the fundamental challenge of information management. There are two elements of situational awareness: information and skill. Information is provided by the staff and major subordinate commands in the form of feedback to help build the commander's understanding of the situation. Skill is the personal understanding of the situation that is based on the commander's experience, judgment, and intuition. The combination of information and skill provides the commander with an image of the situation from which he can base future decisions.

Raw Data

Raw data are the facts and individual pieces of information (data) that are the building blocks of processed information. This initial class of information

is rarely of much use until transformed and processed in some way to give it meaning.

Processed Data

Processed data comes from organizing, correlating, comparing, processing, and filtering raw data and making it readily understandable to the potential user. The act of processing gives the information a limited amount of value. Processed data may have some immediate, obvious, and significant tactical value but it has not been evaluated or analyzed.

Knowledge

Knowledge is the result of analyzing, integrating, and interpreting processed data; it brings meaning and value to a situation or event. Simply put, knowledge is a representation of what is happening.

Understanding

Understanding means we have gained situational awareness and it allows the commander to be better prepared to anticipate future events and to make sound decisions, even in the face of uncertainty. It is the highest level of information and the most valuable. It is an appreciation for why things are happening. Understanding occurs when personnel synthesize bodies of knowledge and then apply experience, judgment, and intuition to reduce gaps generated by uncertainty in order to arrive at a complete mental image of the situation.

Characteristics of Quality Information

Quality information adds value to the decision-making process. Information is susceptible to distortion, both by the enemy (intended) and by friendly sources (unintended). The characteristics of quality information are as follows:

- Accuracy—Information that conveys the true situation.
- Relevance—Information that applies to the mission, task, or situation at hand.
- Timeliness—Information that is available in time to make decisions.
- Usability—Information that is in common, easily understood formats and displays.
- Completeness—Information that contains all the necessary information for the decisionmaker.
- Brevity—Information that has only the level of detail required.
- Security—Information that has been afforded adequate protection where required.

Information Format

Sight is the most used human sense and 75 percent of all environmental stimuli are received through visual reception. The retention rate of graphic presentations is greater than that of verbal presentations. Whether visual, textual, or verbal, the presentation format should be commonly understood and used consistently to minimize confusion and facilitate understanding. The staff produces information in a format that is tailored to the commander's needs; for example, some commanders prefer visual products, yet other commanders prefer textual information, while still others may prefer a combination of several products. It is important for the staff to clearly learn which form of information is most useable to the commander. It is equally as important for the commander to identify to the staff the format he finds most useful.

Focusing Information Management

Information management focuses the flow of information shown in figure 1-2. The staff and major subordinate command process, commander's critical information requirements (CCIRs), and commander's judgment are tools that can be used to focus large volumes of available data to permit the efficient flow of quality information through the information hierarchy. Commanders and their staffs use these tools to focus and sort information in order to identify information that satisfies critical information requirements linked to key decisions. The commander's intent, commander's guidance, and CCIR are used to measure the effectiveness of information that is used to support decisionmaking.

Commander's Intent

MCWP 5-1, *Marine Corps Planning Process*, states, "Commander's intent is the commander's personal expression of the purpose of the operation. It must be clear, concise, and easily understood. It may also include how the commander envisions achieving a decision as well as the end-state or conditions, that when satisfied, accomplish the purpose."[1] The commander's intent establishes the standards by which success is judged. Through commander's intent the aims of the commander are articulated, his information requirements can be discerned, and the framework for effective information management is formed.

Commander's Guidance

The commander's guidance forms the basis for planning, execution, and direction; therefore, it must be clear and concise. Although not prescriptive in nature, the planning guidance assists the staff in making initial judgments on the ways and means to achieve a decision. Based on his personal experience and judgment, the commander articulates clear and concise guidance that helps to focus the information management efforts of the staff and subordinate commanders.

Commander's Critical Information Requirements

CCIR are tools for the commander to reduce information gaps generated by uncertainties that he may have concerning his own force, the threat, and/or the environment. They define the information required by the commander to better understand the battlespace, identify risks, and to make sound, timely decisions in order to retain the initiative. CCIR focus the staff on the type and form of quality information required by the commander, thereby reducing information needs to manageable amounts. Instead of reacting to the threat, commanders are able to maintain tempo by controlling the flow of information they require to attain the level of understanding they need within the battlespace. As events unfold, information requirements may change as new decisions are required and CCIR are continuously assessed for relevance to support current and future decisions/situations. The commander approves CCIR, but the staff recommends and manages CCIR to assist the commander.

The commander categorizes CCIR as either friendly activities, threat activities, or the environment. Friendly activities CCIR include the information the commander needs to make timely and appropriate decisions relevant to his force. This includes such information as force closure, critical supply levels, and levels of combat effectiveness. Threat activities CCIR include the information the commander needs at a particular time that relates with other available information and intelligence to assist in assessing and understanding the situation. This includes indications and warnings of threat intent and/or actions by the threat (e.g., troop movements, changes in opposing force intents or policies). Environment CCIR include the information the commander needs regarding the physical battlespace environment. This includes all types of information not covered in the friendly or threat categories (e.g., meteorological conditions, supporting infrastructure, geopolitical considerations, relevant activities of nongovernmental and private organizations).

Decisionmaking

Assessment

MCDP 6 establishes the doctrinal foundation and the conceptual framework for assessment:

> The commander commands by deciding what needs to be done and by directing or influencing the conduct of others. Control takes the form of feedback—the continuous flow of information about the unfolding situation returning to the commander—which allows the commander to adjust and modify command action as needed. Feedback indicates the difference between the goals and the situation as it exists. . . . Feedback is the mechanism that allows commanders to adapt to changing circumstances—to exploit fleeting opportunities, respond to developing problems, modify [plans], or redirect efforts.[2]

Assessment is the final step in the PDE&A cycle. The PDE&A cycle is the process the commander and staff use to plan operations, make accurate and timely decisions, direct effective execution of operations, and assess the results of those operations. It is a framework that supports the commander's efforts to assimilate information in the chaotic environment of war in order to increase tempo through timely and decisive actions.

Assessment answers the commander's question, "How are we doing?" It should help the commander identify success or failure, determine the extent to which required conditions have been met for follow-on action, and recognize when a particular endstate has been reached. More specifically, assessment (the evaluation of effects) should enable the commander to measure the overall progress of an operation as it unfolds on the battlefield. By accurately measuring this progress, the commander can make informed decisions for future actions.

The assessment process is continuous throughout planning and execution. Planning is where the commander establishes his intent (purpose) for the mission as well as his envisioned endstate. It is also where the staff identifies the essential tasks and associated conditions that must be accomplished in order to achieve mission success. These are amplified and supported by measures of effectiveness (MOEs), indicators, and pertinent information in the commander's order that are expressed in clear, precise, and accurate language. They may be used as "gauges" to measure performance in execution and become information requirements for evaluating the effectiveness of previously made decisions.

Understanding Information

The commander must frequently make decisions with incomplete information—less than perfect understanding. He may make decisions based on partial understanding or at a limited level of situational awareness. Understanding is used to support decisions and is a basis for future planning and execution. Understanding can affect decisions already made and allow the commander to better visualize success or failure. Experience, personality, and intuitive reasoning by personnel making the decisions

often influence the type and form of information used to achieve understanding. The development of tasks, conditions, MOEs, indicators, and pertinent information can be useful tools to recognize quality information used to achieve understanding.

Tasks

There are two parts to any mission: the task to be accomplished and the reason or intent behind it. The task describes the action to be taken. If tasks are to be assessed, planners must develop proper task statements. Tasks that are developed must have a corresponding purpose that describes effects in tangible and measurable terms. Generally, these effects can be described in terms of time, sizes of units, observable capabilities, or terrain. Once a purpose is identified and some tangible qualifiers in terms of time and terrain are identified during planning, assessing the degree to which the task has been accomplished during execution is easier.

Conditions

A condition describes the status of battlespace elements that the commander would like to have in place before executing a decision. It can also be used to determine when a task, stage, or phase of an operation is complete. Conditions must be tied to tasks. Conditions are expressed in enough detail to allow personnel to realistically assess progress, yet broad enough to provide commanders the flexibility to adjust actions to meet unexpected changes. Conditions must be understandable, relevant, and measurable in order to be effective assessment tools. Conditions are expressed as a positive statement rather than a negative statement to enable personnel to realistically assess the status of associated battlespace characteristics.

Measures of Effectiveness

MOEs are those characteristics of the battlespace that comprise specific components of a condition. MOEs support highly specific information needs. Often MOEs identify desired results to support a key decision that satisfies the components of a condition. MOEs are defined in terms of indicators and pertinent information. The establishment of MOEs enable the commander to assess whether or not conditions have been satisfied, which allows the commander to evaluate whether or not decisions have achieved the desired results.

Indicators

Indicators are measurable observations that show that the MOEs are, or are about to be, satisfied. Indicators are supported by one or more pertinent information criteria used to evaluate the supported MOE. Traditionally, each staff section identifies and monitors specific indicators. This procedure can result in the same indicator being managed by multiple staff sections. A better approach is to ensure all staff sections are aware of all indicators associated with each MOE. Sharing this information can prevent staff sections from duplicating efforts to satisfy the same indicator. More than one indicator can support MOEs, a condition, and/or a CCIR.

Pertinent Information

Information needed to satisfy indicators is identified as pertinent information. Pertinent information satisfies indicators that are established relative to each MOE used to support a desired condition or CCIR. Staff sections identify information they need to satisfy each indicator for which they are responsible. Timely identification of pertinent information enables the staff to efficiently allocate resources in order to routinely produce quality information. Even more importantly, it is the tool that enables the information management officer (IMO) to work with each staff section to create an information management plan (IMP) that identifies procedures used to facilitate the delivery of quality information to those who need it in a format they can quickly understand.

Planned Decisions

Planned decisions are developed during the planning phase and implemented during execution. Decision points are generated/created as a result of the planned decision process. Decision points identify points in time or space where the commander expects to make key decisions. Friendly and enemy forces and environmental factors influence those key decisions. Understanding the type of information necessary to support planned decisions enables the unit to implement effective and efficient information management procedures. These procedures enable the commander and staff to clearly identify what type of information is required, who needs it, when it needs to be shared, and the required format. To support planned decisions, the commander and the staff will—

- Develop decision points during planning that will influence actions and events during execution. The decision support matrix (DSM) and decision support template (DST) list these decision points and any associated named areas of interest.
- Establish CCIR that identify friendly, threat, and environmental information the commander requires to gain the knowledge needed to make key decisions listed in the DSM and DST.
- Establish indicators to help determine whether the MOE has been met.
- Develop named areas of interest, based on geographic locations, that intelligence collection assets monitor to confirm or deny enemy activity/indicators for the appropriate threat CCIR. Report requirements are determined for subordinate commands that support friendly, threat, and environmental CCIR.
- Ensure that information that satisfies an indicator is immediately sent to the combat operations center, flagged as input to a CCIR, and immediately shared with all other staff sections. If the indicator provides knowledge the commander needs to satisfy the CCIR, the staff

is notified and the commander decides whether or not he has adequate understanding of the situation to make a decision.

Figure 1-3 demonstrates how personnel can identify and manage quality information to support planned decisions based on warfighting functions. As indicators occur and understanding develops, the senior watch officer consults the DSM/DST to determine what preplanned solutions are still valid. These facts are then placed before the commander, who applies his experience, judgment, and intuition to the information to make a decision.

Spontaneous or Unplanned Decisions

Information management must be flexible enough to provide information that supports both planned and spontaneous decisions for which no prior planning was conducted. Spontaneous or unplanned decisions are those decisions generated by unexpected or unplanned actions or activities. Since combat is inherently uncertain, the commander and the staff use course of action (COA) wargaming to identify environmental factors and threat activities that could affect the friendly COA, and to develop branch plans to address these possibilities. Potentially, planners

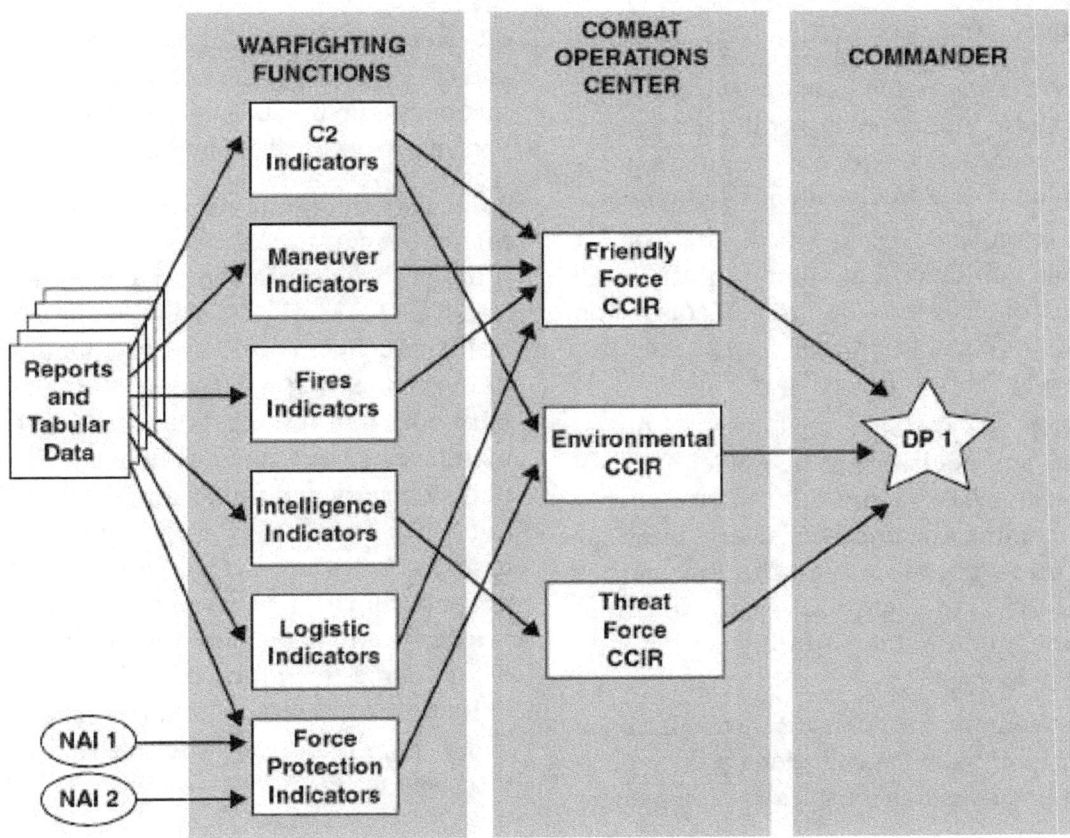

Figure 1-3. Managing Information to Support Planned Decisions.

could develop multiple branch plans; they could be intimately aware of friendly, threat, and environmental actions, reactions, and counteractions; and they could still be surprised. When the plan is executed, the threat could perform an unexpected action or activity that would require a completely new branch plan to be developed and executed. However, armed with the knowledge and understanding gained by developing numerous branch plans, the commander and staff planners are now better prepared to observe, orient, and react with "unplanned" decisions. Knowledge and understanding of current and anticipated actions by the threat, friendly forces, and the environment enables the commander to make sound, timely decisions that control tempo even in the face of uncertainty. The following actions may occur in support of unplanned decisions:

- Indicators are generated as an event develops. Some of these indicators are collected and reported in accordance with commander's guidance and intent as articulated during planning.

- As this information is reported, the combat operations center will at some point in time recognize that an event is occurring that is not on the DSM/DST and for which no planning has been done.

- Recognition of an unplanned event requires new plans and decisions to be made. This action generates new information requirements from the commander and staff. These information requirements focus on the impending event indicators to determine timing, location, disposition, and/or status of the event and its probable outcome.

- An understanding of the event is developed once sufficient information is collected on the indicators. This understanding enables the commander to make an informed decision and control tempo despite unexpected events.

Information Management During Joint, Combined, and Multinational Operations

Information management procedures must be capable of providing a framework for rapid and effective exchange of information that enables the Marine Corps component to share critical and relevant information in support of joint, combined, and multinational operations. Although each Service possesses Service-unique capabilities, joint operations require information management procedures that are commonly understood by all components/Services. Effective information management procedures ensure all essential information requirements and the processes necessary to support those information requirements are understood by each component supporting the joint force.

Joint force commanders and component commanders maintain their situational awareness through the use of a common operational picture (COP). The Marine Corps component and subordinate echelons of command maintain a common tactical picture (CTP). The COP and CTP help commanders execute the single battle by maintaining situational awareness. The CTP displays friendly and threat forces in a graphic format with amplifying text as required. It also displays relevant tactical control and fire support coordination measures. The CTP and COP are derived using a common tactical dataset and other sources of information. The common tactical dataset consists of shared information derived from numerous sources that support the COP and CTP.

CHAPTER 2
PERSONNEL AND DUTIES

Personnel are the second element of command and control. This chapter identifies the principal managers of quality information within each command and outlines their information management responsibilities. Although these individuals are key personnel with specific information management duties, every user of information has an inherent responsibility to help manage, filter, and fuse information. In a personnel-constrained environment, information management personnel may serve multiple roles and provide expertise to numerous functional areas (i.e., staffs, boards, and cells). In every command, all personnel, as information users, should support information management procedures that enhance decisions made throughout the decision cycle.

Key Information Management Personnel

Commander

The commander does not merely participate in planning: he drives the process. His intent and guidance are key to planning. The commander uses planning to gain knowledge and situational awareness to support his decisionmaking process. Subordinate commanders use the commander's guidance and concept of operations to accomplish the mission. The commander establishes priorities for gathering and reporting quality information needed to maintain situational awareness and achieve a level of understanding. Clear guidance, commander's intent, and CCIR provide a focus for the staff to identify quality information used to support key decisions.

Additionally, the commander performs the following information management functions:

- Approves the command information management plan used to share quality information.
- Approves the command communications plan that complements and supports the information management plan.

Chief of Staff/Executive Officer

The chief of staff/executive officer is responsible for coordinating the actions of the staff and ensuring that the commander receives the information he needs to make decisions. The chief of staff/executive officer directs the development of the operation order and performs the following additional information management functions:

- Directs the development of and approves the daily battle rhythm.
- Implements the IMP.
- Appoints the IMO.
- Ensures that information management procedures are adequately shared with the staff and subordinate commands.

Primary Staff

The staff functions as the commander's eyes and ears. They take the commander's guidance, intent, and CCIR and use them to collect, filter, and analyze data. The staff then provide the resulting information to the commander. The principal staff members perform the following information management functions:

- Identify pertinent information used to support the daily battle rhythm.

- Establish internal staff section procedures to share quality information through the use of newsgroups, e-mail, message handling, home-pages, requests for information (RFI), and suspense control measures.
- Appoint a staff section information manager as a point of contact for information management matters.
- Appoint personnel responsible for maintaining information technology and network infrastructure used to share quality information.
- Ensure training is completed for basic information management and security procedures for appropriate personnel in each staff section.
- Evaluate information management procedures to assure efficient flow of quality information.
- Establish benchmarks and conduct subjective analysis to evaluate efficiency and effectiveness of information management procedures.
- Work closely with the IMO to develop network diagrams that identify the functional applications and network infrastructure required to share quality information with those that need it in a format that is clearly understood.

Information Management Officer

The IMO must be capable of working closely with personnel of all ranks to coordinate procedures necessary to share quality information generated by the staff. These procedures should promote development and exchange of knowledge required by the commander to make decisions. At a minimum, the IMO must be aware of the following functional needs:

- Key decisions the commander must make to successfully achieve desired results. These decisions are normally reflected in a DSM.
- Knowledge required by the commander to achieve the level of understanding he needs before making key decisions.
- Information the commander needs to reduce his uncertainty about his force, the threat, and the environment. Normally this information satisfies the CCIR.

- Information required to satisfy established conditions for tactical operations.
- Information the commander needs on a daily basis to maintain situational awareness.

To perform these functional needs, the IMO must be capable of working closely with the staff to accomplish the following tasks:

- Develop and publish the command IMP.
- Determine processes and procedures to satisfy CCIR.
- Publish and update the information management matrix.
- Develop daily battle rhythm matrix (DBRM) (see the Daily Battle Rhythm Matrix paragraph on page 3-3).
- Coordinate additional training required by staff and component elements to support production of quality information through effective information management procedures.
- Work closely with the command CTP manager (as described in the paragraph entitled Common Tactical Picture/Common Operational Picture Manager on page 2-3) and with staff, subordinate, and higher headquarters IMOs to develop effective, efficient track management procedures.
- Work closely with information exchange technology personnel to facilitate efficient dissemination of quality information throughout the MAGTF.

Staff Section Information Managers

Each staff section information manager should be aware of information required by the commander, when it is required, and the desired format. Staff section information managers are expected to perform the following tasks:

- Monitor internal and external flow of information by their staff section.
- Ensure the command IMO is aware of routine daily updates and information produced by each staff section to satisfy CCIR.

- Provide the G-6/S-6 a daily update of command-level information requirements that may need network infrastructure support, sharing of information, and equipment to support functional needs (i.e., the number and type of equipment, internet protocol [IP] accounts, e-mail and computer naming conventions, radio net and telephone requirements, and user lists for inclusion in e-mail and telephone directories).
- Ensure compliance with information management procedures used to share quality information through the use of Intranet/Internet capabilities.
- Coordinate and conduct information management training for internal staff section members.

Request for Information Manager

RFIs are used to reduce uncertainty within the command. Questions that cannot be satisfied by organic assets are forwarded to higher headquarters in the form of a formal RFI. Answers to questions that allow the staff to promote knowledge they require to support the commander are shared through RFI responses. RFI managers are assigned by the G-2 for intelligence-related questions and the G-3 for all nonintelligence-related questions. RFI managers are expected to perform the following tasks:

- Receive, validate, prioritize, and submit RFIs to the appropriate authority for resolution.
- Develop/manage a tracking system that ensures that RFIs are processed in a timely manner and that responses are expeditiously disseminated to the requester and accessible to all personnel.

See the Networks paragraph on page 3-9 for more discussion of RFI procedures.

Common Tactical Picture/ Common Operational Picture Manager

The CTP/COP manager is responsible for the reporting and display of friendly, threat, and other appropriate tracks. He is also the unit track manager. The CTP/COP manager for blue force tracks is normally assigned by the G-3. The CTP/COP manager for enemy force tracks is normally assigned by the G-2. The overall unit CTP/COP manager normally is the G-3 CTP/COP manager. The CTP/COP manager is expected to perform the following tasks:

- Coordinate and deconflict all ground unit tracks with all major subordinate commands and higher headquarters. Air tracks are the responsibility of the aviation combat element, which provides air tracks to the command element as required.
- Work closely with the senior watch officer to ensure that the location and disposition of friendly and enemy ground units are visually updated as required.

Webmaster

Internets and Intranets are valuable resources used to share quality information both internal and external to the staff. The webmaster, who is assigned by the G-6, creates a unit's web site. Specifically, the webmaster is responsible for the following tasks:

- Create the command web site to support sharing of quality information. At a minimum, the web site supports internal and external reporting requirements, CCIR, RFIs, commander's daily brief, and daily battle rhythm.
- Maintain the web site to ensure that changes to information requirements are posted in a timely manner.
- Maintain security over the web site and ensure that information contained therein is available to the appropriate personnel.
- Ensure procedures are developed, disseminated, and understood on how to access the site, upload information, and change the site.
- Maintain links to external sites of interest to the staff.
- Develop formatting standards.
- Create initial pages for each staff section and train representatives from each section on how

to maintain their page in order to ensure uniformity of design among sections.

● Develop custom web-based applications.
● Advise/assist staff section web representatives.

Subordinate Unit and Higher Headquarters Information Management Officers

Each major subordinate command and higher headquarters appoints an IMO as a primary point of contact for information management matters. Subordinate and higher headquarters IMOs can be expected to perform the following tasks:

● Review/update information reflected by the reports matrix and daily battle rhythm.
● Conduct liaison with the higher headquarters and adjacent IMOs.
● Coordinate and assist the training required to produce quality information throughout the Marine air-ground task force (MAGTF).
● Ensure appropriate management personnel are designated within the command to address technical support if the MAGTF chooses to use automated or electronic means to share and manage command information (i.e., web site, newsgroup, public folders, shared directories).

Organizations That Influence Information Management

Combat Operations Center, Tactical Air Operations Center, and Combat Service Support Operations Center

The combat operations center, tactical air operations center, and combat service support operations center support current operations. Personnel operating in these centers conduct the following information management related activities:

● Assess information flow to support operations.
● Review and record incoming message traffic to filter and fuse information in accordance with the commander's guidance and intent. Provide the commander with information that relates to the CCIR and decision points.
● Manage the CTP through commonly understood track management procedures.
● Monitor the CTP's efficiency, effectiveness, and accuracy to provide enhanced situational awareness of friendly and enemy forces.
● Maintain a master suspense action log/journal.
● Maintain a chronological record of significant events.
● Direct production of the commander's daily briefings and fragmentary order production.
● Assess, update, and integrate priority intelligence requirements.

Combat Intelligence Center

The combat intelligence center is the overarching intelligence operations center established within the main command post. It performs the following functions:

● Reviews, assesses, and disseminates threat-related information in a format that is quickly understood by those needing the information. This provides a common understanding of the threat within the designated battlespace.
● Monitors the efficiency, effectiveness, and accuracy of the threat assessment determined by the common tactical picture parameters.
● Works closely with the combat intelligence center, future operations section, and future plans section to ensure threat assessments satisfy designated planning horizons and are updated accordingly.
● Develops, monitors, and updates priority information requirements and RFIs. Responds to priority information requirements and RFIs of the commander, staff, and subordinate commands.

Future Operations Section

The future operations section develops courses of action that support the next stage or phase of the operation, and information management supports the following activities:

- Collaborative planning, which requires the sharing of quality information through the use of collaborative capabilities and commonly understood procedures as outlined in appendix A.
- Visually displaying information, which includes tools and overlays that describe fire support coordinating measures, boundaries, maneuver, logistics/sustainment, decisions, and intelligence.
- Planning tools that are capable of supporting COA development.
- Filtering tools and procedures to assess measures of effectiveness for conditions tethered to key decisions required to support execution and transition to the next stage or phase of the operation.

Future Plans Section

The future plans section develops the next phase of the operation. Information management supports the following future plans activities and tools:

- Collaborative planning, which requires the sharing of critical and relevant information through the use of collaborative capabilities and commonly understood procedures.
- Visually displaying information, which includes tools and overlays that describe fire support coordination measures, boundaries, maneuver, logistics/sustainment, decisions, and intelligence.
- Planning tools that are capable of supporting the development of the next phase of the operation.

Security Personnel

Information Security Manager

The information security manager is responsible for the proper accountability, control, personnel access, and physical security/storage of noncompartmented classified data (hard and soft copy forms). This includes the TOP SECRET control

officer's responsibility for the JTF TOP SECRET registry's accountability, control, and access.

Special Security Officer

The special security officer is responsible for sensitive compartmented information (SCI) management, control, and access and is normally a G-2/S-2 function.

Information Systems Security Officer

The information systems security officer is responsible for safeguarding the command's information systems. The information systems security officer enhances the command's information security knowledge, skills, and abilities through command-wide education and training programs. The information systems security officer performs the following information management functions:

- Maintains a plan for site security.
- Ensures the information system is operated, used, maintained, and disposed of in accordance with security policies and practices.
- Conducts site survey and vulnerability assessments of systems in order for them to process classified and sensitive information.
- Ensures the information system is accredited and certified if it processes sensitive information.
- Ensures users and system support personnel have the required security clearances and authorization, and are familiar with internal security practices before access to the information system is granted.
- Ensures the information system has intrusion detection devices.
- Enforces information system security policies and safeguards.

Operations Security Officer

The operations security officer provides oversight and implementation of the command operations security program, ensuring protection against compromise of friendly force information. This position is normally a G-3/S-3 function, and it receives support from the G-2/S-2 (counterintelligence officer).

User Responsibilities

The following duties and responsibilities are incumbent upon all users of information to ensure proper information flow:

ı Report information as required by the command CCIR.
ı Ensure accuracy and relevance of information before further dissemination. Clearly differentiate between original information and previously reported information to avoid duplicate reporting.
ı Properly control, classify, protect, and archive all information and information systems for which they are responsible. This requires a clear understanding of approved control measures for various classifications of information.
ı Read and comply with the information requirements published by the IMP.
ı Retain any irrelevant or conflicting information discarded during analysis and correlation of data—do not destroy it prematurely. This information may become useful when combined with additional facts.

CHAPTER 3
COMMAND AND CONTROL
SUPPORT STRUCTURE DEVELOPMENT

C2 support structure is the third element of command and control. C2 support structure is more than advanced technology and equipment—it is the integrated use of organizations, people, capabilities, training, procedures, doctrine, and network infrastructure to support C2 and decisionmaking processes. An effective C2 support structure produces information that promotes understanding of the situation or event and allows the commander to be better prepared to direct and coordinate actions in the execution of a decision.

Information Flow

An effective C2 support structure improves information flow by—

- Reducing labor and saving time by automating repetitive procedures and performing intensive calculations.
- Disseminating information to many users in different geographic locations.
- Transforming tabular data into graphic or other visual products that allow personnel to quickly understand the situation or event. Appendix A contains examples of visual mapping products that support each step of the Marine Corps Planning Process.

When developing a C2 support structure that enhances the flow of information across warfighting functions (command and control, maneuver, fires, intelligence, logistics, force protection) and across traditional staff section boundaries, numerous factors should be considered. These factors include location of information, mobility, accessibility, filter/fusion, and push versus pull.

Location of Information

The repositioning of the required information at anticipated point(s) of need speeds up the flow of information, reduces demands on communications networks, and provides required information to those that need it in a timely manner. Knowing that information is prepositioned at a specific point is critical when units are highly dispersed.

Mobility

A reliable and secure flow of information must be commensurate with the commander's mobility and tempo of operations requirements. The capabilities and procedures necessary to support effective information flow must be flexible enough to adjust immediately to support low footprint and highly mobile command posts, as well as the mobility requirements of subordinate units.

Accessibility

All levels of command must have access to the information they require to support concurrent and/or parallel planning, mission execution, and assessment. An effective C2 support system uses automation to provide the user with quality information quickly; for example, automated, dynamic visual display of forces in a CTP environment.

Filter/Fusion

Information is received from many sources, in many mediums, and in different formats. Filtering occurs when information is evaluated/assessed and deemed to be of value and irrelevant data is discarded. Fusion is the logical blending of information from multiple sources into an accurate, concise, and complete summary. The C2 support structure must give analysts and decisionmakers the ability to quickly filter and fuse information.

Push Versus Pull

Information management uses two basic approaches to share information: supply-push and demand-pull. The C2 support structure incorporates the most appropriate approach based on the commander's information requirements.

A supply-push methodology relies heavily on information being pushed from the source to the user, either as the information becomes available or according to a schedule. The advantage of supply-push is that the commander normally does not need to request quality information. Quality information is delivered (or pushed) to the user in a timely manner. This type of information management can result in information overload because producers of information may not completely understand user information requirements.

In a pure demand-pull system the user initiates the flow of information and seeks out information required. If the information is readily available—pre-existing in a database—the requirement is quickly satisfied. If the information is not available, the requirement must move through the chain of command until it reaches the appropriate level. Information can be tailored specifically to support the identified requirement, thereby avoiding overload. The disadvantage to the demand-pull system is the cost in time, since the search for information may not begin until the commander or user has identified a need.

Information Management C2 Support Structure

The development of an information management C2 support structure consists of the following three steps: process flow, configuration flow, and personnel requirements.

Process Flow

MCDP 1-2, *Campaigning*, identifies six basic warfighting functions: command and control, maneuver, fires, intelligence, logistics, and force protection, and an information process supports each warfighting function. Each process captures the step-by-step tasks necessary to collect, analyze, and disseminate the information. Understanding the process flow (how information is physically transmitted and processed) that supports each warfighting function enables the IMO to work closely with the staff and commander to develop effective information management procedures. An effective C2 support structure accounts for the different warfighting processes unique to each level of command.

The first step in the development of an information management C2 support structure is to identify the process flow that supports each warfighting function. A process flow diagram identifies the series of tasks necessary to support each warfighting function. Information management is central to the process and is focused on supporting the processes that satisfy information requirements essential to the warfighting functions.

Configuration Flow

Once the process flow diagrams have been created, the next step in the development of an information management C2 support structure is the development of the configuration flow diagrams. A configuration flow diagram describes the configuration of systems necessary to support the tasks in the process flow diagram.

A configuration flow diagram is established by performing the following actions—

- Determining the system required to perform each task identified by the process flow diagram.
- Identifying the network infrastructure necessary to disseminate information produced by personnel performing each task identified by the process flow diagram.

Each system is placed in the appropriate command element organization linked by the proper network infrastructure. Current command relationships and task organization of forces are taken into consideration to develop the configuration flow diagram. This methodology permits a command to identify system and network shortfalls or potential vulnerabilities.

Personnel Requirements

In the final step of developing a C2 support structure, the command identifies personnel requirements from the configuration flow diagram and determines the number of personnel, skill sets (training), and procedures necessary to support each warfighting function. The identified personnel requirements are then measured against what is currently being used by the command. This comparison allows the command to identify any deficiencies and to implement corrective action if necessary. Both of these actions result in an efficient flow of information within the command C2 support structure and effective decisionmaking.

Documentation

Capturing information management decisions and plans in documentation that is easily distributed facilitates a common understanding of information management throughout the command.

Information Management Matrix

The information management matrix records all information requirements, user(s), recipients, capabilities used to process the information, and pathways necessary to pass information. It is a powerful planning tool used to support execution, to determine the source of information flow problem(s), and to correct any information flow problems through appropriate action/coordination. A carefully designed information management matrix significantly enhances the efficiency and effectiveness of staffs and decisionmakers. The staff

determines the content of the information management matrix.

Daily Battle Rhythm Matrix

The DBRM is a schedule of key daily events that involve the commander and the staff. These events can include staff briefings, updates, visits, reports, and products (e.g., air tasking order, intelligence summary). These events are extracted from the information management matrix and placed on the DBRM. The purpose of the DBRM is to disseminate the schedule and facilitate the integration of various events. The commander and the staff are responsible for identifying which event needs to be placed on the DBRM. The chief of staff/executive officer manages the DBRM.

Decision Support Matrix

The DSM links information to key decisions and helps the commander coordinate activities and maintain situational awareness. The commander and staff develop a DSM during the planning process. The DSM identifies key decisions that the commander expects to make during the next stage or phase of the operation. Table 3-1, on page 3-4, illustrates how a DSM can be used to assist with the identification of quality information used to support assessment. Once the DSM is written, a DST can be created. The DST is a mapping product that graphically displays the text information contained in the DSM.

The DSM identifies the CCIR needed by the commander in order to gain knowledge and to achieve the understanding he needs before making key decisions to achieve the desired results. The DSM identifies conditions and MOEs to assist in recognizing when desired results for each decision are achieved. For certain decisions, MOEs and approved conditions may be the same, but that determination depends upon the type of decision being made by the commander. The DSM identifies indicators that support each MOE. Indicators may be developed to support the designated condition directly. Each staff section identifies pertinent information used to support

Table 3-1. Example of a Decision Support Matrix.

Decision	Task	CCIR	Condition	MOE	Indicators	Pertinent Information	NAI	Collection Plan	TAI
Attack the 3d Regimental Artillery Group (RAG) to prevent it from disrupting the heliborne assault on LZ Bluebird.	Neutralize the 3d RAG.	What is the capability of the 3d RAG to mass fires against our heliborne assault?	The 3d RAG is unable to mass fires at or above the battalion level on LZ Bluebird from H-hour to H+36.	No massed fires observed from 3d RAG units within 30 km of LZ Bluebird for 48 hours prior to H-hour.	Volume and accuracy of artillery fire within 30 km of LZ Bluebird decreased.	Number of artillery rounds from within 30 km of LZ Bluebird.	4	Unit SHELREPs; Counterbattery radar reports.	3
				No observed reinforcement of 3d RAG units for 72 hours prior to H-hour.	Vehicular traffic on 3d RAG lines of communications decreased.	Number of vehicles travelling on 3d RAG lines of communications.	7	BDA from MAW missions, unmanned aerial vehicles, artillery forward observers.	5

each indicator. Indicators are managed using tools that enable all personnel to share pertinent information that satisfy indicators. Staff sections ensure the IMO is aware of pertinent information used to satisfy indicators.

Request for Information Management

RFIs are specific, time-sensitive ad hoc requirements for information or products submitted to higher headquarters to support an ongoing crisis or operation not necessarily related to standing requirements or scheduled intelligence production. RFIs are generated to answer questions that cannot be resolved with organic assets, when the information does not exist within internal databases, and when the information cannot be satisfied by resident subject matter experts. Figure 3-1 depicts a typical process flow used to support RFI management.

Information Manager

An RFI manager (G-2 or G-3) serves as the central point of contact for multiple sources: the operational planning team, primary staff sections, and major subordinate commands. All RFIs are submitted to the appropriate RFI manager who validates the RFI, assigns priorities, and submits the RFI for resolution. Each RFI manager applies the commander's guidance and intent, CCIR, and good judgement to guide validation and prioritization of each RFI. RFIs directly tied to the CCIR are assigned a higher priority than other RFIs.

Submission Guidelines

Before the requestor submits an RFI, local information and the RFI database is searched to ensure that the information is not available or that a similar request has not already been submitted. If the information cannot be found, an RFI is submitted to the appropriate RFI manager. All intelligence-related requests for information are processed through a G-2 RFI manager. All nonintelligence-related requests for information are processed by the G-3 RFI manager. The following guidelines apply to the drafting and submission of RFIs:

- Limit the RFI to one question per request. Multiple questions can increase response time and add confusion as multiple agencies answer the questions from one RFI.

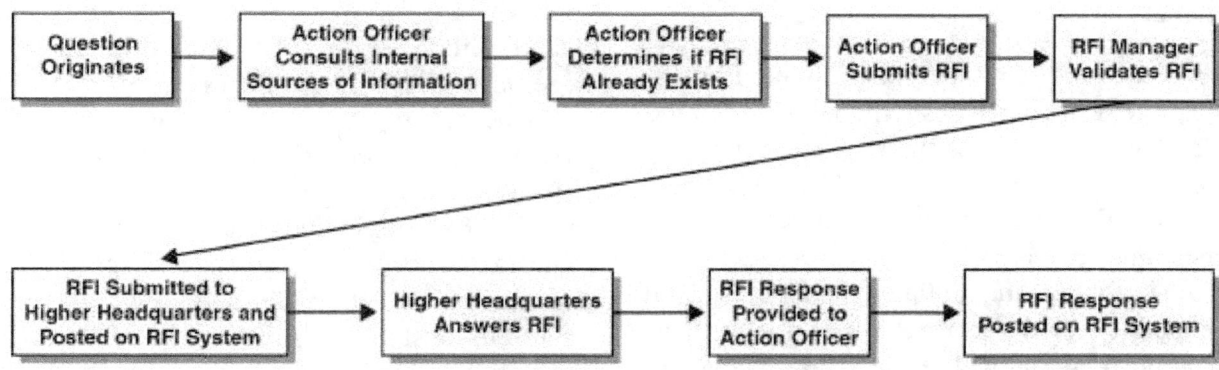

Figure 3-1. RFI Process Flow.

● State the RFI as a specific question. Provide sufficient detail so that the receiving action officer completely understands the request and the nature of the requirement.

Validation

Once an information requirement is identified, the action officer checks locally available resources, including other staff officers, other command sections, on-line services (libraries, databases, repositories), and other organizations (higher, adjacent, subordinate, supporting). If the information requirement cannot be satisfied locally, the action officer submits the request to the appropriate RFI manager for resolution. Upon receipt, the RFI manager screens the requirement to determine validity. Valid RFIs are recorded, managed, tracked, and sent to higher, subordinate, or adjacent headquarters or to another agency to obtain the requested information. The validation process includes, but is not limited to, the following:

● Determining if the requested information is resident within the command.

● Determining which agency should receive the RFI for action.

● Approving the request. If approved, submit RFI. If not approved, the request should be returned to the originator for appropriate justification.

● Assigning a tracking number to all validated RFIs.

● Logging in the RFI on the RFI tracking sheet and posting the RFI to the MAGTF RFI database. If there is a duplicate request, the RFI manager provides all originators with the appropriate RFI tracking number.

● Forwarding the request to the appropriate headquarters, staff sections or agency for action and confirming receipt of the request by the action addressee.

Submission to Higher Headquarters

Once validated, the RFI manager generates an RFI to higher headquarters that contains the approved, formal command RFI. Only the RFI manager is authorized to submit the RFIs to higher headquarters. All other information requests that are generated through normal staff action to higher headquarters are not RFIs and should not be labeled as such. Following this submission process reduces formal RFIs to only those that warrant command-level attention and are critical to planning or execution. Upon receiving information that satisfies a RFI (i.e., via message or report from higher headquarters or an outside agency), the RFI manager immediately transmits the response to the originator of the RFI. Additionally, the RFI manager updates the status for that RFI on the RFI tracking system.

Responses

RFI responses are sent to the respective RFI manager. The RFI manager posts the response to the RFI database and notifies the requester that a response has been received. The RFI tracking log is updated to reflect that a response was received and that the requester was notified. It is the responsibility of the individual that initiated the RFI to screen the response and determine if it is adequate or whether an additional RFI needs to be generated to acquire the desired information. If the RFI is not answered completely or additional information is desired, the requestor should resubmit the RFI with appropriate comments or clarification.

Major Subordinate Command Procedures

Major subordinate commands manage RFIs within their command. Upon confirming that an information requirement is critical to planning or execution and that the information requirement cannot be satisfied at their level, major subordinate command RFI managers submit their RFI to their higher headquarters for resolution.

Information Management Plan

The IMP expresses how the command will manage and control information. The IMP reflects all three elements of C2: information, people, and C2 support structure. The IMP assigns responsibilities and provides instructions for personnel who will manage information. Information management responsibilities identified by unit standing operating procedures (SOP) do not need to be duplicated in the IMP. Development of an IMP is a vital step to ensure that decisionmakers have the information they require, when they need it, and in a format that they can quickly understand. Each command must develop an IMP tailored to manage its information in the context of its mission and the current situation or event.

An effective IMP provides guidance to ensure that quality information is provided to those who need it in a form that they can quickly understand. The IMP should include information management filtering tools; unique information management personnel needs (duties, responsibilities, and skill requirements); C2 support structure requirements (processes and procedures); and information management system protection. The IMP should include specific guidance for management of the CTP/COP, the collaborative planning system, RFI management procedures, and network applications used to share critical and relevant information. The IMP may be distributed by the use of newsgroups, web pages, or other applications.

The development and execution of an effective IMP requires the participation and interaction of all staff sections. Once each staff section identifies their information requirements, warfighting process and configuration flow diagrams, and personnel requirements, the appropriate information is incorporated into the IMP.

Information management policy and procedures are top-down in nature and the IMP must include considerations for joint interoperability. Commanders and staffs at all levels must have a common understanding of the joint information management policy and procedures. JTF information management practices nest within those already established by the supported combatant commander. Component, MAGTF, and major subordinate information management practices are required to nest within those of the JTF. Appendix B provides a list of tools and references that will support execution and the development of the IMP.

Networks

Information is transmitted over five specific networks: Joint Worldwide Intelligence Communications System (JWICS), SECRET Internet Protocol Router Network (SIPRNET), Nonsecure Internet Protocol Router Network (NIPRNET), allied networks, and coalition networks. The JWICS is a classified network used to process and disseminate information classified as SCI. The SIPRNET is a classified network authorized to process and disseminate information classified as SECRET or below.

The NIPRNET is a sensitive but unclassified network able to process and disseminate sensitive information that is identified as unclassified or below. Allied networks are established and maintained by our allies and are made available to U.S. forces to maintain interoperability when conducting operations. Control measures are normally the same as that of all information releasable to that allied nation. Combined forces establish coalition networks as required to support a specific operation. The JTF commander and appropriate classification authorities determine the control measures used to protect and disseminate classified information disseminated by a coalition network.

CHAPTER 4
SECURITY

Technology allows us to deliver accurate information in a timely fashion; however, the enemy is also able to use technology to compromise the security of our information. To safeguard against unauthorized access or modification of information, each command must detect and protect against information compromise. The security of information is critical to information management and the effective conduct of operations. Proper security enables commanders to sustain tempo by monitoring the status of friendly information, identifying any attempts to penetrate or attack friendly force information, and to identify the location and type of threat involved. Armed with that information, commanders can determine appropriate passive or active measures to deter further intrusion or initiate actions to deceive or possibly terminate the threat as appropriate. The security goal of information management is to maintain and ensure integrity of information within the command.

Information Assurance

Information assurance is the joint term applied to those security actions taken to protect friendly information and information systems. It is all "information operations that protect and defend information and information systems by ensuring their availability, integrity, authentication, confidentiality, and non-repudiation. This includes providing for restoration of information systems by incorporating protection, detection, and reaction capabilities."[1]

Information Protection

Mission accomplishment depends on protecting information and information systems from destruction as well as safeguarding against intrusion and exploitation. Therefore, a key component of the IMP is information protection. Information protection is addressed through command security programs; e.g., physical security, information security, computer security, and communications security. All users share responsibility for information protection. Information security is a force protection issue and all users should be extremely vigilant in the use of any form of communication. It is imperative to use established security protocols and procedures for successful mission accomplishment. There are three steps to defeating a network intruder:

- First, prepare a defense. Network defenses provide limited, not complete, protection. It is possible for an intruder to acquire information that could be detrimental to friendly force operations/mission objectives.
- Second, defeat the intruders. Network detection devices identify when and where an intrusion attempt occurs and the method of intrusion.
- Third, establish a contingency plan that meets and defeats the threat and restores essential capabilities within the time constraints established by the commander. This capability allows the commander to choose when and where to degrade, defeat, deceive, or possibly destroy the threat once it is detected.

Information can only be protected through a comprehensive plan to defend against, detect, deceive, and defeat hostile intrusion. The IMO must work closely with the staff to ensure that critical databases and networks are adequately protected.

Threats

Threats are potential violations of security and exist because of vulnerabilities in a system. There are two basic types of threats: accidental threats and attacks.

Accidental Threats

An accidental threat occurs if information is exposed unintentionally or if modifications to the system leave it vulnerable to attack. Exposures can emerge from hardware and software failures as well as user and operational mistakes. For example, an exposure occurs when a user sends confidential mail to the wrong person.

Attacks

An attack is an intentional threat to violate system security and destroy, modify, fabricate, interrupt, or intercept data. An attack results in disclosure of information, a violation of information confidentiality, or in the modification of the system, which results in a violation of system integrity. Examples of attacks are viruses, worms, Trojan Horses, denials of service, and hackers.

Viruses

A computer virus, by definition, is any program (or code) that replicates itself by attaching a copy of itself to another file. A virus is particularly dangerous because users typically do not know that their functional capabilities or networks are being infected until the virus reveals itself (the consequences of which can range from annoying

to catastrophic.) Viruses are a more common source of infection as modem/Internet file transfers become more commonplace. NIPRNET, SIPRNET, and JWICS systems are becoming more popular as a file and e-mail transfer medium, and users of these systems are at greater risk than other network users because these systems bypass network server virus protections.

At the most basic level, viruses can be categorized as one of two types: file or boot. File viruses reside inside .exe or .com files, gain control of the computer system when that file is executed, and attach a copy of themselves to other files after they gain control. Boot viruses reside in the section of the floppy disk or hard disk that is loaded into memory at boot time, and hence, are loaded into memory before other programs. This enables book viruses to re-infect floppy disks inserted in the disk drive. The following subsets of file viruses resist easy detection:

- Stealth viruses avoid detection via file size monitoring in various innovative ways that exploit disk operating system (DOS) interrupts.
- Polymorph or mutation viruses copy modified versions of themselves each time they spread to other files.
- Macro-type viruses infect everyday document and spreadsheet files. This virus type exploits the small macro executable code inside word processing or spreadsheet files and is spread through e-mail attachments and is the most infectious virus.

Worms

A computer worm is a self-contained program (or set of programs) that spreads functional copies of itself or its segments to other computer systems (usually via network connections). Unlike viruses, worms do not need to attach themselves to a host program. There are two types of worms: host computer worms and network worms.

Trojan Horse

A Trojan Horse is a program or file that appears to be useful and harmless, but it has harmful side effects such as destroying data or breaking security on the system on which it is run. It is similar to a virus except that it does not propagate itself as a virus does.

Denial of Service

A denial of service attack is not a virus but a method hackers use to prevent or deny legitimate users access to a computer. Denial of service attacks are typically executed using DOS tools that send many request packets to a targeted Internet server (usually web, file transfer protocol [FTP], or mail server), which floods the server's resources, making the system unusable. Any system that is connected to the Internet and equipped with tactical control protocol (TCP)-based network services is subject to attack.

Hackers

A hacker is a person who breaks into, attempts to break into, or uses a computer network or system without authorization.

Protection

The first tier of threat detection and elimination occurs at the server level. Typically, a server is a more powerful computer that stores and accesses data; receives, transmits, and routes e-mails; and performs processing tasks on behalf of a user's computer. The G-6/S-6 is responsible for server protection and network system administrators manage protection at the server level. The network system administrator programs the server to run anti-virus software automatically at the server level to scan for viruses or infected files on the shared drive. However, servers are also susceptible to compromise and some viruses can bypass server protection and infect a user's computer. Therefore, the second tier of defense occurs at the user's computer.

At the user level, all workstations should have anti-virus software that detects and eliminates viruses when the user boots up the system. The user can also elect to run the anti-virus software to perform a virus check on a hard drive or floppy disk. Combat operations run 24-hours a day, therefore, virus detection and anti-virus software must be initiated at least once daily, and users should initiate a virus check at the start of each shift.

The last tier of virus detection and elimination is the individual diskette. Diskettes, which move from machine to machine, can easily host viruses and infect each machine they are used in. Unless you know otherwise, assume diskettes are infected. The user is responsible for scanning diskettes with virus detection software before the diskette is used.

Information Security

Information security is "the protection of information and information systems against unauthorized access or modification of information, whether in storage, processing, or transit, and against denial of service to authorized users. Information security includes those measures necessary to detect, document, and counter such threats. Information security is composed of computer security and communications security."[2]

Access to Classified Information

The information security manager establishes procedures to verify security clearances for assigned and augmented personnel. Access, regardless of clearance, is based on a "need to know" basis that is consistent with operational requirements and is controlled by the individual who has authorized possession, knowledge, or control of the information. Cleared personnel should not be permitted access to classified information and information systems until briefed on information management and information security procedures.

Security Marking of Documents

All users must ensure they properly mark all documents with the appropriate classification level. Header and footer markings should be included as well as paragraph markings, even though some viewers do not display header and footer text. Do not rely solely on header and footer comments for proper marking of electronic documents.

Computer Disk Classification

Diskettes are registered/labeled with the appropriate operational classification. They are labeled with either the SF 710 (1-87) UNCLASSIFIED sticker (green) or the SF 707 (1-87) SECRET sticker (red). Diskettes used in a SECRET computer system, regardless of the classification of the files on the diskette, are classified SECRET and marked appropriately.

Classified Destruction

Classified material that is no longer required for operational purposes are disposed of in accordance with the U.S. Code, Title 44, *Public Printing and Documents*: chapter 21, "National Archives Records and Administration" and chapter 33, "Disposal of Records;" SECNAVINST 5510.30A, *Department of the Navy Personnel Security Program*; and SECNAVINST 5510.36, *Department of the Navy (DON) Information Security Program (ISP) Regulation*.

Material identified for destruction is protected as appropriate for its classification until it is actually destroyed. The method of destruction must eliminate the ability to reconstruct the classified information. Dispose of written materials via an authorized shredder (crosscut is preferred) or by placing it in a burn bag. Shredders are the preferred method of destruction. Burn bags should be placed throughout the unit workspace, particularly areas that include printers and copiers, and are controlled in a manner that minimizes the possibility of unauthorized removal of their classified contents prior to actual destruction. Diskettes and removable hard drives are physically destroyed to prevent unauthorized access to the classified material recorded upon them. If diskettes and hard drives are still useful use authorized degaussing and erasure programs to remove classified material and render the diskettes and hard drives reusable. Records of destruction are not required for SECRET material except for NATO and foreign government documents. Two signatures are required on the record of destruction for NATO or foreign government SECRET material. Records of destruction are not necessary, unless required by the originator, for CONFIDENTIAL material. See the unit information security manager or SCI special security officer if there are any questions regarding destruction of classified materials.

Future, Multi-Level Security Requirements

The competing demands of security and wide dissemination of information require databases and networks with different levels of classification and access. Currently, the different networks include the NIPRNET, the SIPRNET, and the JWICS. However, in any given scenario a command may also need to operate on an allied- or coalition-classified network. Passing information from a network to another network of higher classification is usually achievable and secure. However, sharing information from a protected network to another network of a lower classification is much more difficult and is currently not possible in an automated fashion. Operators must take great care to ensure that information protected at the higher level is not compromised and inadvertently placed into the network with a lower classification. Operators can use local procedures to manually verify that information is appropriate for release, and then use some manually managed procedure (i.e., copying to a known clean disk and moving that disk to the network of lesser classification) to disseminate the information.

The ability to exchange various classifications of information between different networks on one workstation is not currently authorized. As a result, organizations are required to use redundant systems to perform the same functions conducted at different classification levels. As an example, the all-source fusion center requires three different workstations to perform intelligence assessment: one terminal to access SCI; one terminal to access SECRET information; and one terminal to collect, analyze, and disseminate open-source information. Once multi-level workstations are approved to process and disseminate different classifications of information, the use of redundant systems to support information requirements will be reduced.

APPENDIX A
INFORMATION MANAGEMENT'S
SUPPORT OF PLANNING

Planning is based on the commander's intent and guidance and requires immense amounts of focused information to be successful. Information management tools and procedures provide commanders and planners the information they need in a form that they can quickly understand. Information management tools and procedures also facilitate the exchange of information throughout the command, which in turn enhances the ability to plan at all levels of command and promotes unity of effort throughout the MAGTF.

The Marine Corps Planning Process establishes procedures for analyzing a mission, developing and analyzing COAs against the threat, comparing friendly COAs against the commander's criteria and each other, selecting a COA, and preparing an operation order for execution. The MCPP organizes the planning process into six manageable and logical steps (see fig. A-1). It provides the commander and staff a means to organize their planning activities and to transmit the

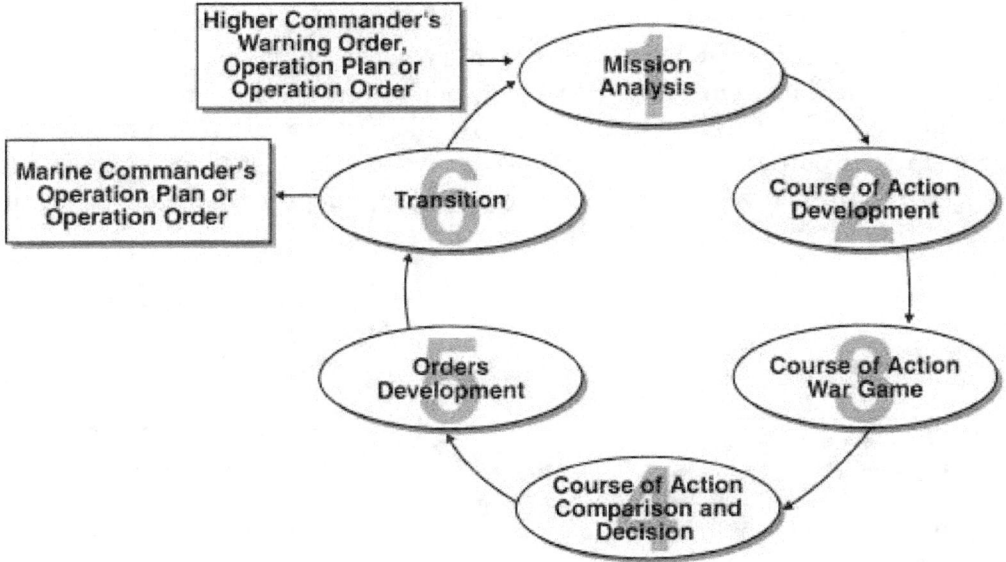

Figure A-1. The Marine Corps Planning Process.

plan to subordinates and subordinate commands. Through this process, all levels of command can begin their planning effort with a common understanding of the mission and commander's intent. Interactions among the various planning steps allow a concurrent, coordinated effort that maintains flexibility, makes efficient use of time available, and facilitates continuous sharing of critical and relevant information. See MCWP 5-1 for a detailed discussion of the Marine Corps Planning Process.

With a thorough understanding of higher headquarters' orders and intent and an understanding of their own commander's battlespace area evaluation (CBAE) and initial guidance, planners identify and use products that record the specified, implied, and essential tasks that support current information management requirements and capabilities. Staff estimates are continuously updated and provided to planners using various forms of information, to include voice, text, and visual display products. Throughout the planning process, planners maintain situational awareness of current operations by monitoring a dynamic visual display of the CTP that depicts current status of friendly and threat forces and relative environmental concerns. This appendix provides examples of information management tools, procedures, and an explanation of how they can be used to support each step of the planning process.

Mission Analysis

The purpose of mission analysis is to review and analyze orders, guidance, intent, and other information provided by higher headquarters to produce a unit mission statement. This step forms the foundation for the remainder of the Marine Corps Planning Process. Figure A-2 illustrates the basic input, the process, and the output for mission analysis. Information management tools and procedures, discussed in the following paragraphs, can assist in the development and dissemination of mission analysis products.

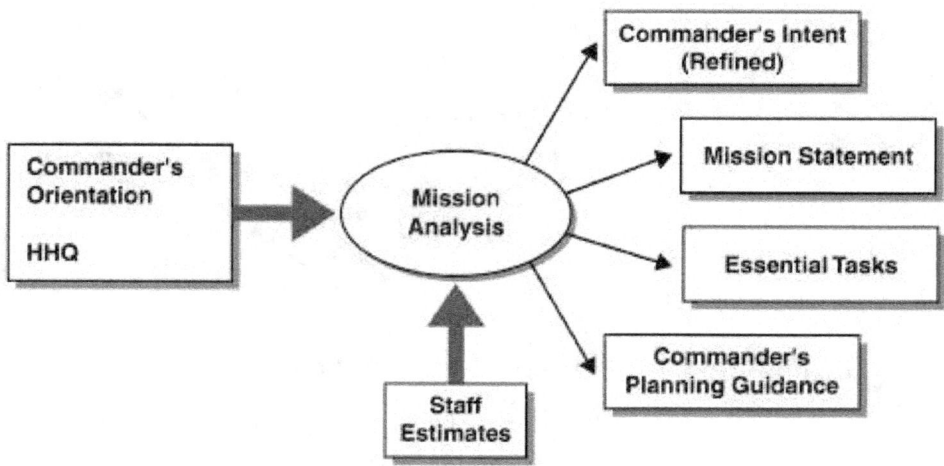

Figure A-2. Mission Analysis.

The commander's vision, which is based on his understanding of the mission, battlespace, the threat, and the environment, is contained in the commander's battlespace area evaluation (CBAE). The commander uses the CBAE to develop, assess, and communicate knowledge to the staff to support all four aspects of the decisionmaking process (i.e., planning, decision, execution, and assessment). Figure A-3 is an example of the CBAE created in text form through the use of information management tools. This electronic form can then be disseminated to numerous personnel simultaneously.

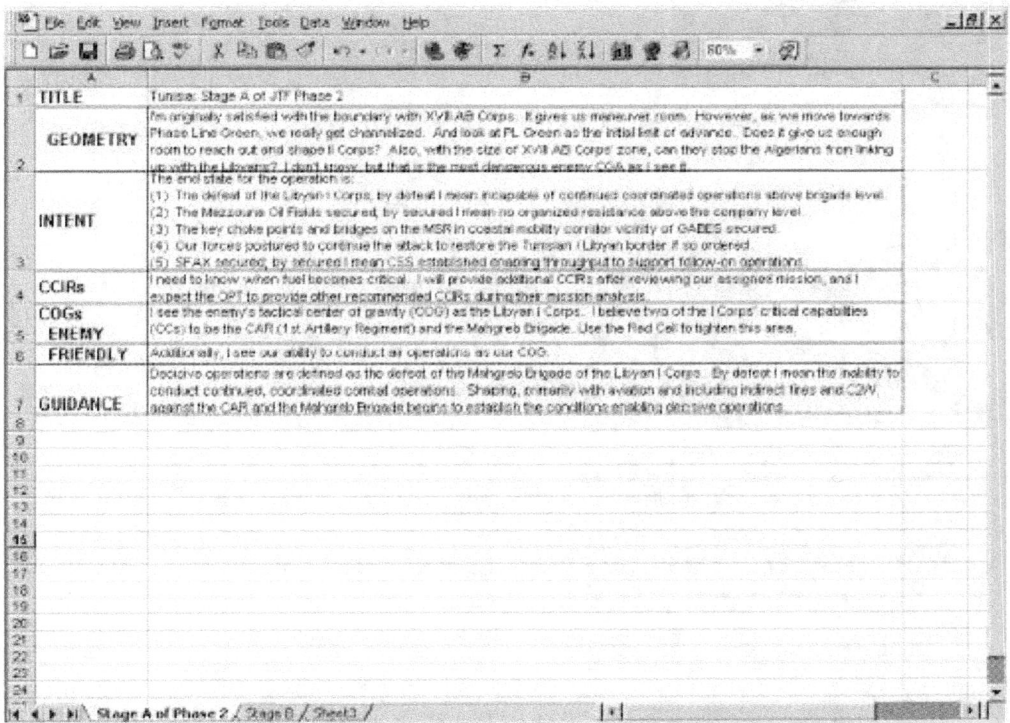

Figure A-3. Recording Commander's Battlespace Area Evaluation.

Figure A-4, on page A-4, is an example of how current capabilities combine graphic display products and text to record the CBAE. This information can then be electronically disseminated to numerous personnel simultaneously. The originator possesses the ability to control access and dissemination.

Using collaborative tools, MAGTF planners record text information that describe the commander's orientation, which includes higher headquarters plans, orders, estimates, availability and suitability of forces, and results of personal reconnaissance. Automated graphic display mapping capabilities are used to record analysis of the threat and associated intelligence preparation of the battlespace (IPB) products, to include environmental concerns. Figure A-5, on page A-4, shows how information management tools display text and graphic products created during mission analysis.

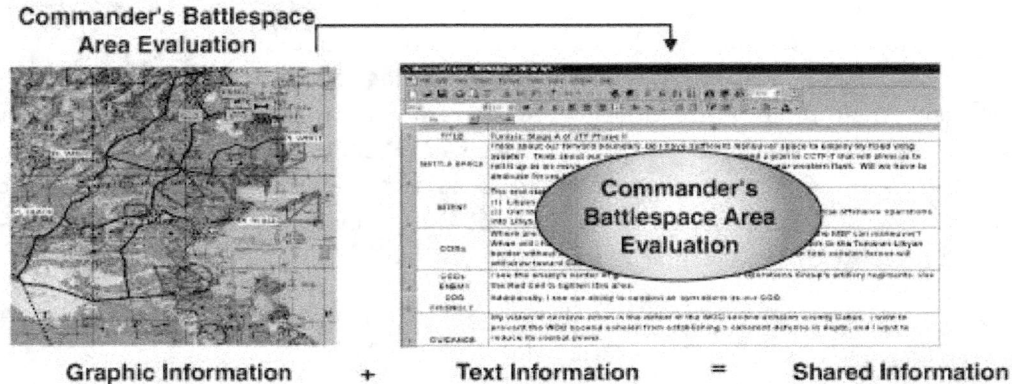

Graphic Information   +   Text Information   =   Shared Information

Figure A-4. Graphic Display Product.

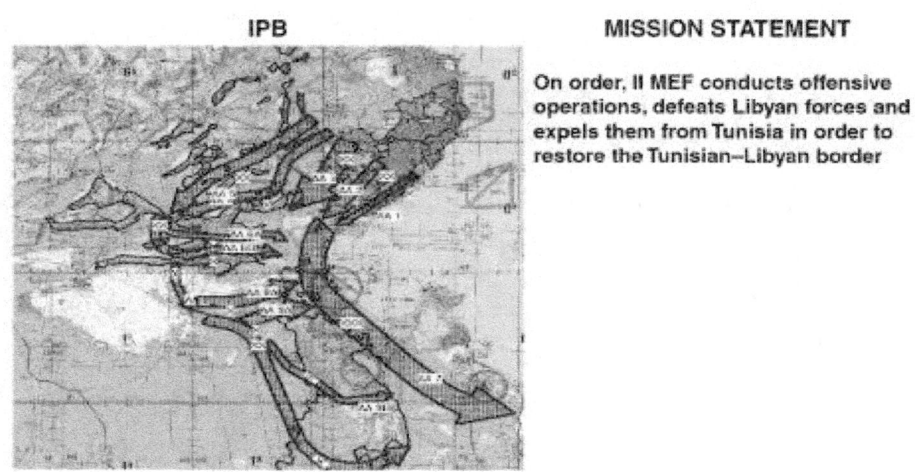

IPB

MISSION STATEMENT

On order, II MEF conducts offensive operations, defeats Libyan forces and expels them from Tunisia in order to restore the Tunisian–Libyan border

Figure A-5. Example of Mission Analysis Products.

Course of Action Development

The mission statement, commander's intent, and commander's planning guidance are used to develop several COAs that are suitable, feasible, acceptable, distinguishable, and complete with respect to the current and anticipated situation, the mission, and the tasking/intent from the higher headquarters commander. Figure A-6 illustrates the basic input, the process, and the output for COA development.

During COA development, information management tools (e.g., command and control personal computer [C2PC]) and procedures are used to record specified tasks, implied tasks, essential tasks, warning orders, restraints and constraints, assumptions, resource shortfalls, subject matter duty expert shortfalls, centers of

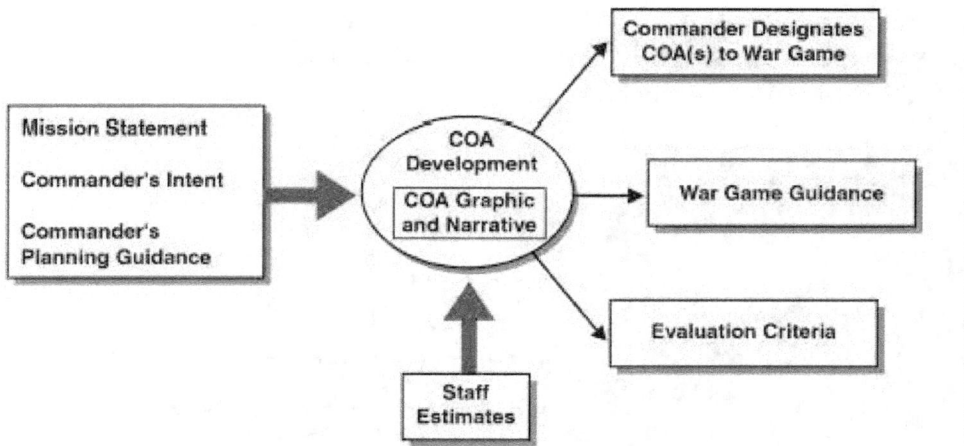

Figure A-6. COA Development

gravity analyses (friendly and threat), CCIR, requests for information, initial staff estimates, and IPB products. Capabilities are tailored to record information for each COA developed. Staff estimates, relative to the time established by the planning horizons for that particular mission, provide planners updated information in both text and graphic display products. These products describe friendly and threat force disposition and array of forces and other pertinent information concerning terrain and weather. Using that information and an array of employment possibilities, planners design a broad plan of how they intend to accomplish the mission, which becomes the COA. Planners can use a combination of information management text and graphic display mapping products to document the following elements of a COA—

- Commander's planning guidance.
- Forms of maneuver.
- Type of attack.
- Designated main effort.
- Requirement for supporting effort(s).
- Scheme of maneuver (land, air, and maritime).
- Sequential and simultaneous operations.
- Sequencing essential task accomplishment.
- Task organization.
- Use of reserves.
- Rules of engagement.

Figure A-7, on page A-6, shows how information management tools display graphic and text information created during COA development.

COA GRAPHIC

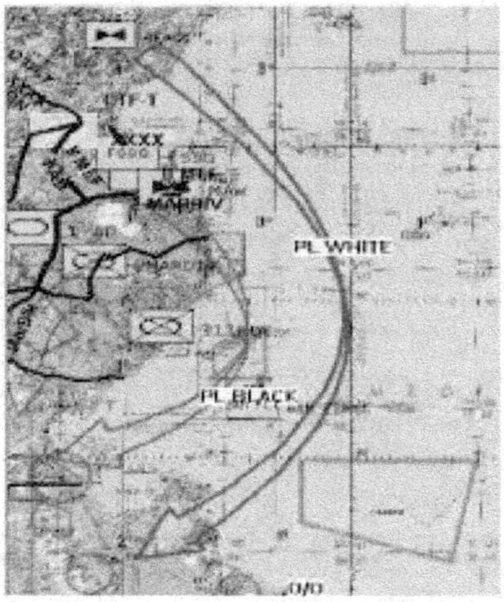

COA NARRATIVE

COA 1: Turning Movement Stage A

II MEF conducts a turning movement to defeat and expel enemy forces in zone in order to restore the Tunisian-Libyan border. This COA is conducted in three phases.

NOTE: During phase B, 6th Fleet conducts amphibious demonstration in support of II MEF.

Stage A: Attack to Gabes:
II MEF attacks with a Marine division, armored division, and Marine air wing.
- The armored division, as the main effort, attacks in zone as the turning force and maneuvers to the west past the WOG's main defensive positions vice Gabes.
- The Marine division attacks to fix the enemy first echelon forces north of Gabes while conducting a linkup with Tunisian forces vice Sfax.

Figure A-7. Example of COA Development Products.

Course of Action War Game

The COA war game involves a detailed assessment of each COA as it pertains to the threat and the battlespace (see fig. A-8). Each friendly COA is wargamed against selected threat COAs. The COA war game assists the planners in identifying relative strengths and weaknesses, associated risks, and asset shortfalls for each friendly COA. Additionally, a COA war game identifies branches and potential sequels that may require additional planning. Short of actually executing the COA, wargaming the COA provides the most reliable basis for understanding and improving each COA, and it allows the staff and subordinate commanders to gain a common understanding of friendly and possible threat COAs. This

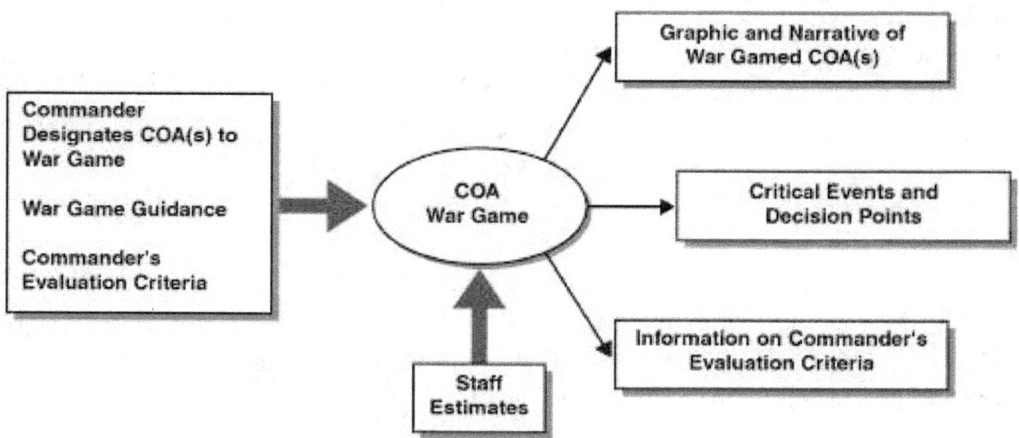

Figure A-8. COA War Game.

common understanding allows personnel to determine the advantages and disadvantages of each COA and forms the basis for the commander's COA comparison and decision.

The commander designates COAs to be wargamed. Using graphic display mapping products, the staff conducts a war game using the threat's most likely, most dangerous, and most advantageous (to friendly forces) COAs. Actions, reactions, and counteractions are recorded in both text and graphic display products. During the war game, the commander's staff and subordinate commands continue to refine their staff estimates and estimates of supportability. Figure A-9 shows how current information management tools display graphic information created during a COA war game.

WAR GAME GRAPHIC   WAR GAME WORKSHEET

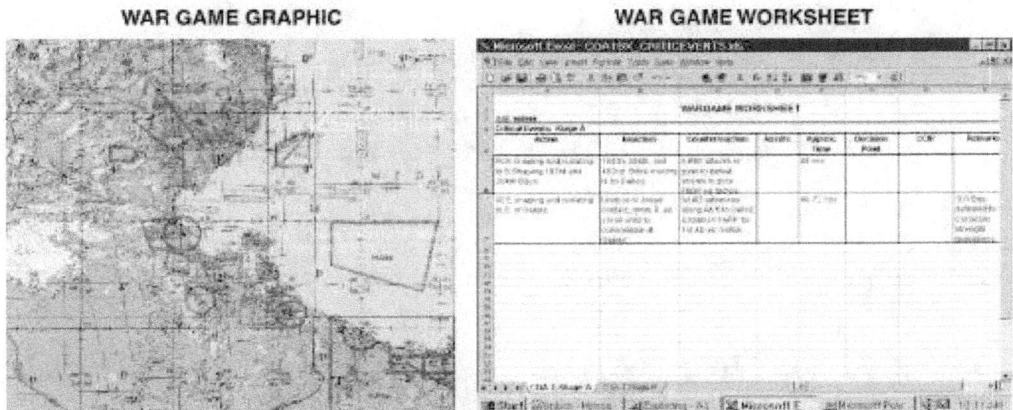

Figure A-9. Example of COA War Game Products.

Course of Action Comparison and Decision

The commander evaluates friendly COAs, first against established criteria, then against each other. Based on this comparison, the commander uses intuitive decisionmaking to select the COA that accomplishes the mission. Figure A-10, on page A-8, identifies the input, process, and output for COA comparison and decision.

COA comparison and decision requires wargamed COAs with graphics and text, a list of critical events and decision points, and information on the commander's evaluation criteria. Other outputs useful in COA comparison and decision may include war game products (e.g., COA war game worksheet, synchronization matrix, event templates, decision support tools), war game results (e.g., initial task organization, identification of assets required and shortfalls, updated CCIR), staff estimates, and subordinate commander's estimates of supportability.

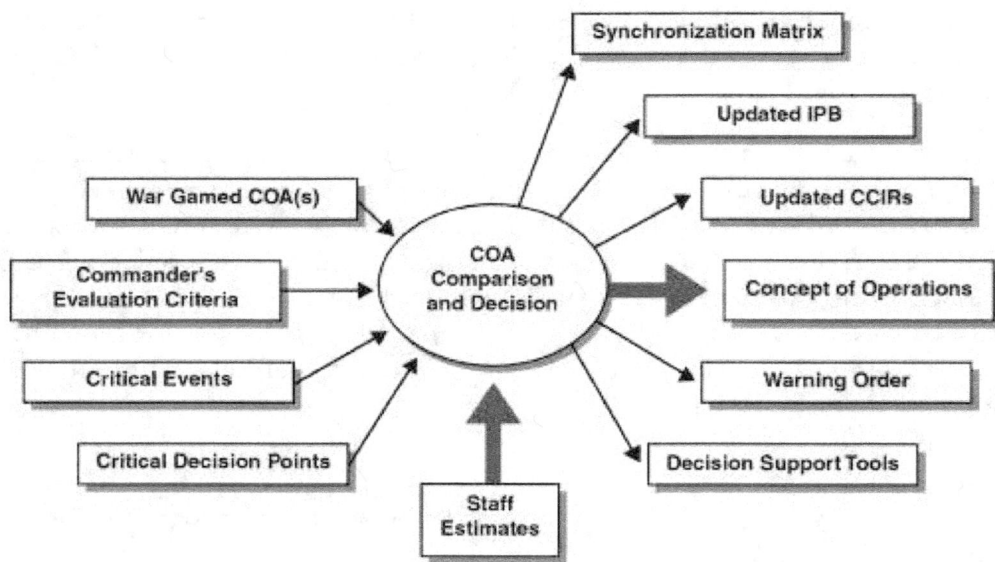

Figure A-10. COA Comparison and Decision.

Figure A-11 shows how information management tools display graphic information created during COA comparison and decision.

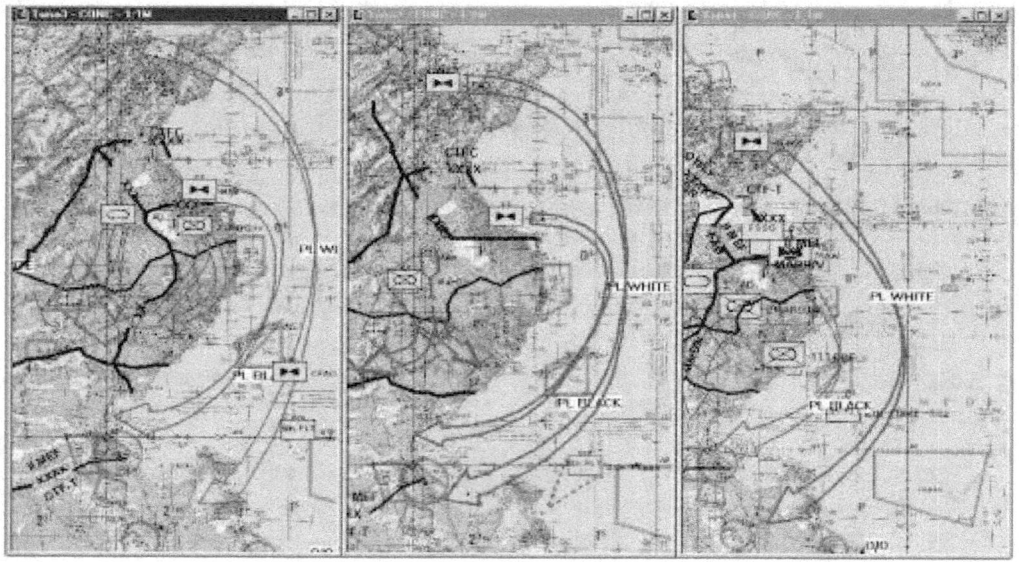

Figure A-11. Example of COA Comparison and Decision Products.

Orders Development

During orders development, the staff takes the commander's COA decision, mission statement, and commander's intent and guidance and develops orders that direct unit actions. Orders serve as the principal means by which the commander expresses his decision, commander's intent, and guidance. Figure A-12 identifies input, process, and output to support orders development.

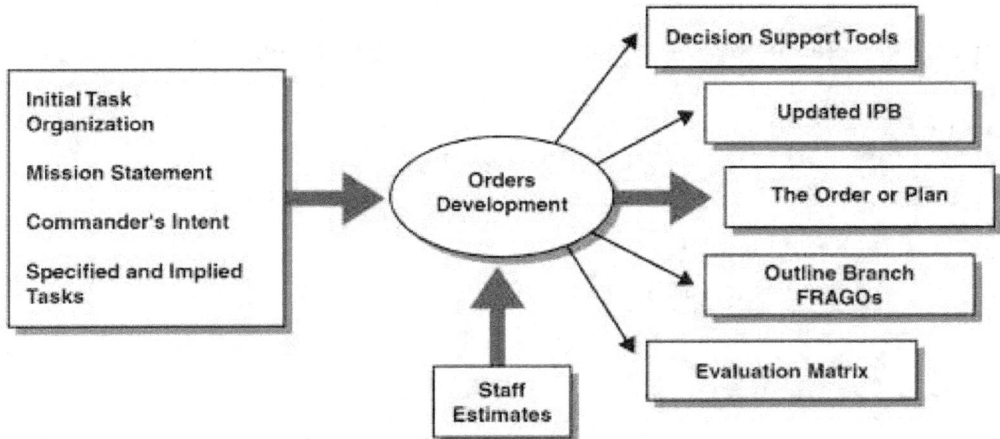

Figure A-12. Orders Development.

The initial task organization, mission statement, commander's intent, concept of operations, and specified and implied tasks, along with the information developed throughout the planning process, form the input for orders development. Other inputs can be recorded using current information management procedures and capabilities, which may include updated intelligence and IPB products, decision support tools, updated CCIR, staff estimates, synchronization matrix, commander's identification of branches for further planning, warning order, existing plans, and SOPs/orders. Figure A-13 shows how currently fielded information management tools (e.g., C2PC) display orders development both as a graphic and as text.

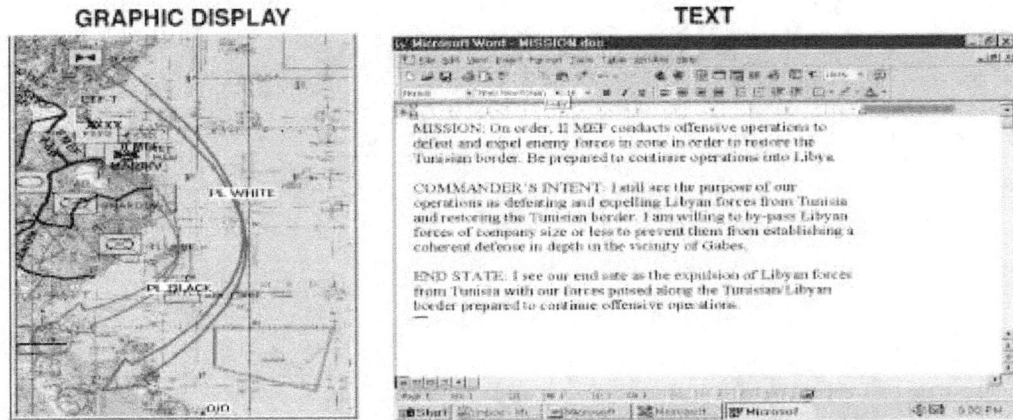

Figure A-13. Example of Orders Development Products.

Transition

During transition, an orderly handover of a plan or order is conducted by those tasked with execution of the operation. Transition provides those who will execute the plan or order the situational awareness and rationale for key decisions necessary to ensure there is a coherent shift from planning to execution. Ideally, one of the planners will accompany the orders to assist staff principles and watch standers understand specifics and gain familiarity with tools and concepts that support the plan and to provide situational awareness. Figure A-14 describes input, process, and output to support transition.

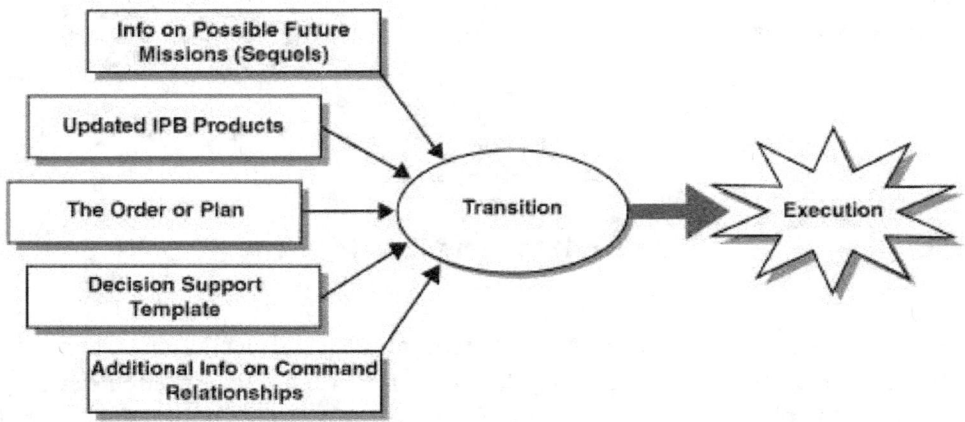

Figure A-14. Transition.

Transition is a continuous process that requires a free flow exchange of information between commanders and staffs to ensure that critical and relevant information is being shared and clearly understood. Information management procedures and capabilities enable personnel to share critical and relevant information through the use of collaborative planning tools, Intranet management, and common tactical picture procedures. Figure A-15 provides examples of transition products that can be created through the use of information management tools.

DECISION SUPPORT MATRIX

DECISION SUPPORT TEMPLATE

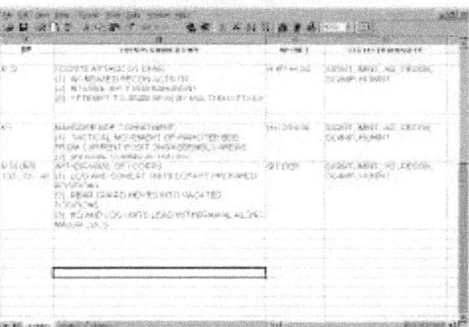
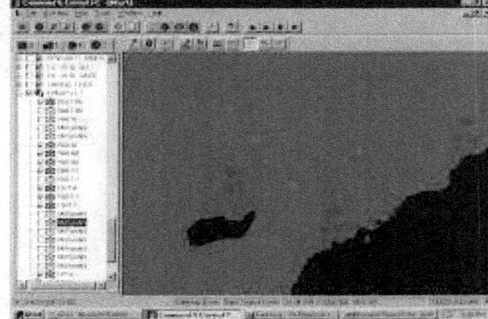

DECISION SUPPORT TEMPLATE

DECISION SUPPORT TEMPLATE

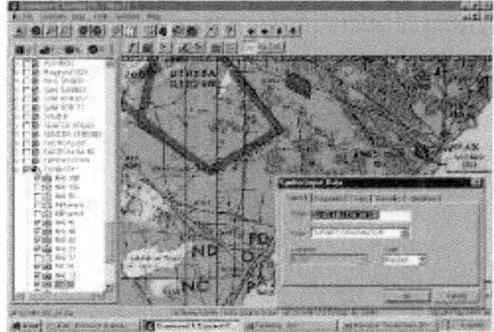
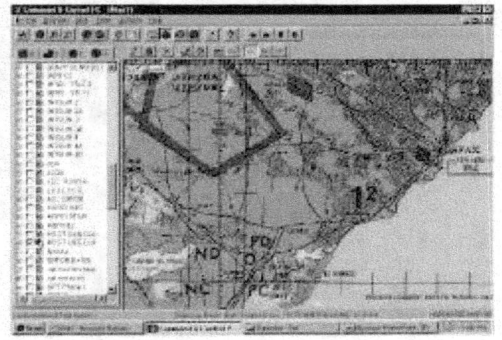

Figure A-15. Examples of Transition Products.

APPENDIX B
INFORMATION MANAGEMENT
TOOLS AND REFERENCES

Execution is the implementation of the plan developed during the planning process. However, no plan is perfect, and modifications must be made as the operation unfolds and the enemy reacts. Accurate and timely information that reflect changes in the battlespace are critical to successful execution of the mission. This appendix discusses information management execution tools and references that support execution.

Execution Tools

Execution tools developed during the Marine Corps Planning Process include the DSM and DST. The DSM provides textual information that identifies key decisions and actions, and it further supports reactions to those decisions and actions. Placing the text information from the DSM in graphic form creates a decision support template. The DST provides a graphic display of key decisions and the actions associated with those decisions. Figure B-1 is an example of how a DST (a graphic product) is created from a DSM (a text product). Placing the DST on the same graphic display capabilities used to maintain a CTP provides each watch officer enhanced situational awareness of key situations or events. These tools enable watch officers to alert commanders of impending key decisions and provide early warning to units executing those decisions.

MAGTF Staff Training Program Pamphlets

Detailed, "how to" information management procedures are being developed and published in pamphlet form by the MAGTF Staff Training Program (MSTP). Each pamphlet will cover a specific information management topic, and it is intended to reflect emerging doctrine that is still under development, but for which the operating forces have expressed a need for interim guidance. These pamphlets can be found on the MSTP web site at http://www.mstp.quantico.usmc.mil/.

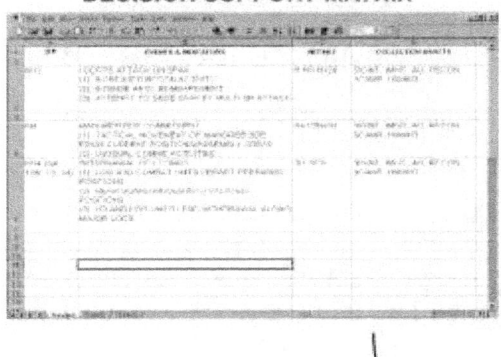

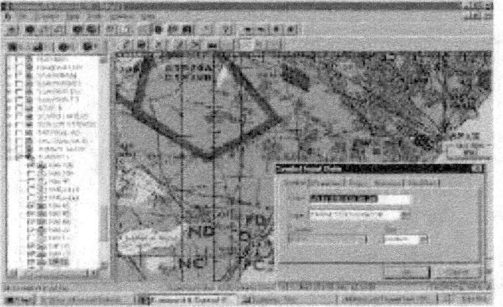

Figure B-1. Example of a DSM Used to Develop a DST.

MSTP Pamphlet 6-1, MAGTF Information Needs

MSTP Pamphlet 6-1 is currently under development. It will identify information needs used to support each echelon of command. These needs will form the foundation for the development of detailed tactics, techniques, and procedures that will describe how information needs will be satisfied by a MAGTF supporting a joint/combined/multinational operation.

MSTP Pamphlet 6-2, Track Management Procedures

MSTP Pamphlet 6-2 is currently under development. This pamphlet will describe the overarching concept of employment for the integrated use of warfighting capability sets used to satisfy MAGTF operations in a joint, combined, or multinational operation. It will describe how the U.S. Marine Corps component and subordinate echelons of command achieve understanding and how the component shares quality information with other components, the JTF, and the combatant command in a COP environment. This pamphlet will identify actions required to achieve understanding of location and disposition of friendly and threat forces within the battlespace and required coordinating measures used to enhance situational awareness. It will also describe how to create and maintain the CTP in a COP environment.

MSTP Pamphlet 6-4, Internets and Intranets in Support of MAGTF Operations

MSTP Pamphlet 6-4 provides staff planners with the techniques and procedures needed to develop effective Intranets and Internets that share quality information needed to support MAGTF operations. This pamphlet discusses collaborative information exchange at the MAGTF staff level; however, the tools and capabilities identified in this pamphlet are also applicable to staffs at all levels. This pamphlet is not a technical manual; consult users manuals and technical manuals for current technical information.

MSTP Pamphlet 6-5, The Planners Guide to C2PC

MSTP Pamphlet 6-5 supplements the C2PC manufacturer's manual by linking C2PC's functionality with Marine Corps specific tasks; e.g., creating IPB overlays, plotting a situation overlay. This pamphlet also identifies how to use C2PC during the Marine Corps Planning Process, in a low intensity conflict/military operations other than war environment, and as a battlefield analysis tool.

MSTP Pamphlet 6-6, LOGAIS in Support of MAGTF Logistics

MSTP Pamphlet 6-6 provides techniques and procedures for employing Logistics Automated Information Systems (LOGAIS) in support of MAGTF operations. It is designed to aid the MAGTF commander and his staff in understanding how LOGAIS supports decisionmaking and the Marine Corps Planning Process. In addition this pamphlet discusses the future development and integration of these systems.

MSTP Pamphlet 6-7, C2 Support to MAGTF Intelligence

MSTP Pamphlet 6-7 focuses on the intelligence cycle used in a MEF-level planning processes. It provides MEF staff action officers with information on current and emerging C2 systems that support intelligence planning and execution and their interface with other related processes and information requirements. It also addresses C2 systems support for conducting intelligence activities and analysis in a MEF combat operations center.

MSTP Pamphlet 6-8, C2 Support for Force Fires

MSTP Pamphlet 6-8 instructs MAGTF commanders and staff officers in the use of current C2 equipment and technology used to plan, execute, and assess fires at the MAGTF level. This pamphlet focuses on the functions, tasks, and processes associated with MAGTF fires and, in particular, the MEF force fires coordination center, but its information is also applicable to the Marine expeditionary brigade (MEB) and the Marine expeditionary unit (MEU). It discusses how the C2 support structure facilitates the actions by the commander and his staff and the management of information in pursuit of understanding and timely decisions. This pamphlet also addresses the capabilities, limitations, and products of C2 equipment and technology and how the MAGTF staff officer can utilize these capabilities and products.

MSTP Pamphlet 6-9, Assessment

MSTP Pamphlet 6-9 defines assessment and provides techniques and procedures that the commander and staff can use when developing their assessment methodology. It addresses assessment as it applies to the MAGTF and major subordinate commands. This pamphlet discusses the conceptual and doctrinal basis for assessment as well as techniques and procedures for staff organization and information management as they relate to the assessment process. Specifically, it identifies how currently fielded capability sets can be used in an integrated manner to reduce uncertainty (RFI management), manage critical information (CCIR management), manage quality information (IMP), and support decisionmaking (DSM/DST) in a CTP supporting a COP environment.

NOTES

Chapter 1

1. United States Marine Corps, MCWP 5-1, Marine Corps Planning Process (Washington, D.C.: Headquarters, U.S. Marine Corps, 2000) p. 2–3.

2. United States Marine Corps, MCWP 6, *Command and Control* (Washington, D.C.: Headquarters, U.S. Marine Corps, 1996) p. 40.

Chapter 4

1. Joint Chiefs of Staff, Joint Publication 1-02, *Department of Defense Dictionary of Military and Associated Terms* (Washington, D.C.: Operational Plans and Joint Force Development, 2001) p. 202.

2. Ibid., p. 203.

Glossary
Section I. Acronyms

AUTODIN . . . . Automatic Digital Network

BDA . . . . battle damage assessment

C2 . . . . .command and control
C2PC. . . . . command and control
personal computer
CBAE . . . . .commander's battlespace
area evaluation
CCIR . . . . commander's critical
information requirement
CJCSI . . . . .Chairman of the Joint
Chiefs of Staff instruction
COA . . . . course of action
COP. . . . . common operational picture
CTP. . . . . .common tactical picture

DBRM. . . . . daily battle rhythm matrix
DIO . . . . defense information officer
DOS . . . . .disk operating system
DP. . . . . .decision point
DSM . . . . decision support matrix
DST. . . . . decision support template

FRAGO. . . . . .fragmentary order
FTP . . . . .file transfer protocol

HHQ . . . . higher headquarters
HTML. . . . . hypertext markup language

IAS . . . . .intelligence analysis system
IMO. . . . . information management officer
IMP. . . . . information management plan
IOW . . . . intelligence operations workstation
IP. .internet protocol
IPB . . . . intelligence preparation
of the battlespace
ISSO . . . . . . information systems security officer

JTF . . . . .joint task force
JP. . . . . .Joint publication
JWICS. . . . . Joint Worldwide Intelligence
Communications System

LOGAIS . . . . Logistics Automated
Information Systems
LZ. . . . . .landing zone

MAGTF . . . . Marine air-ground task force
MAW . . . . .Marine aircraft wing
MCDP. . . . . . Marine Corps doctrinal publication
MCWP . . . . Marine Corps
warfighting publication
MEB . . . . Marine expeditionary brigade
MEF . . . . Marine expeditionary force
MEU . . . . Marine expeditionary unit
MOE. . . . . measure of effectiveness
MRCP . . . . . .Marine Corps reference publication
MSC . . . . major subordinate command
MSTP . . . . MAGTF staff training program

NAI . . . . named area of interest
NIPRNET . . . . nonsecure internet protocol
router network

OIC. . . . . .officer in charge

PDE&A. . . . . .planning, decision,
execution, and assessment

RAG . . . . regimental artillery group
RFI . . . . request for information

SARC . . . . .surveillance and
reconnaissance center
SCI . . . . . . sensitive compartmented information
SHELREP. . . . . shelling report
SIPRNET . . . . SECRET internet
protocol router network
SOP. . . . . standing operating procedures
SORTS . . . . status of resources
and training system
SSO. . . . . .special security officer

TAI . . . . target area of interest
TCP. . . . . .tactical control protocol

U.S.. . . . . United States

SECTION II. DEFINITIONS

commander's critical information requirements—A comprehensive list of information requirements identified by the commander as being critical in facilitating timely information management and the decisionmaking process that affect successful mission accomplishment. The two key subcomponents are critical friendly force information and priority intelligence requirements. Also called CCIR. (JP 1-02)

common operational picture—The integrated capability to receive, correlate, and display a common tactical picture (CTP), including planning applications and theater-generated overlays/projections (i.e., meteorological and oceanographic (METOC), battleplans, force position projections). Overlays and projections may include location of friendly, hostile, and neutral units, assets, and reference points. The COP may include information relevant to the tactical and strategic level of command. This includes, but is not limited to, any geographically oriented data, planning data from the joint operational planning and execution system (JOPES), readiness data from the status of resources and training system (SORTS), intelligence (including imagery overlays), reconnaissance data from the Global Reconnaissance Information System (GRIS), weather from METOC, predictions of nuclear, biological, and chemical (NBC) fallout, and air tasking order (ATO) data. (excerpt from CJCSI 3151.01)

common tactical dataset—A repository of data that contains all the information available to the joint task force (JTF) that will be used to build the COP and CTP. The CTD is not fused, correlated, or processed data in the sense that the information has not been scrutinized by the CINC COP Manager (CCM) or track managers for time value, redundancy, or conflicts. However, the CTD may contain processed intelligence data. The CTD is a major sub-component of the COP and refers to: the CINC designated repository for current battlespace information including disposition of hostile, neutral, and friendly forces as they pertain to US and multinational operations ranging from peacetime through crisis and war for the entire area of responsibility (AOR). Upon discretion of the CINC, the CTD may be a logical database vice physical if there are several JTFs or activities that will necessitate COP reporting. In these cases there may be more than one location of database storage. (CJCSI 3151.01)

common tactical picture—The common tactical picture (CTP) is derived from the CTD and other sources and refers to the current depiction of the battlespace for a single operation within a CINC's AOR including current, anticipated or projected, and planned disposition of hostile, neutral, and friendly forces as they pertain to US and multinational operations ranging from peacetime through crisis and war. The CTP includes force location, real time and non-real-time sensor information, and amplifying information such as METOC, SORTS, and JOPES. (CJCSI 3151.01)

information—**1**. Facts, data, or instructions in any medium or form. **2**. The meaning that a human assigns to data by means of the known conventions used in their representation. (JP 1-02)

information assurance—Information operations that protect and defend information and information systems by ensuring their availability, integrity, authentication, confidentiality, and nonrepudiation. This includes providing for restoration of information systems by incorporating protection, detection, and reaction capabilities. Also called IA. (JP 1-02)

information flow—Term used to describe movement of information. (MCRP 6-23A)

information management—The processes by which information is obtained, manipulated, directed, and controlled. IM includes all processes involved in the creation, collection and control, dissemination, storage and retrieval, protection, and destruction of information. (MCRP 6-23A)

information requirements—Those items of information regarding the enemy and his environment that need to be collected and processed in order to meet the intelligence requirements of a commander. (JP 1-02)

information security—Information security is the protection and defense of information and information systems against unauthorized access or modification of information, whether in storage, processing, or transit, and against denial of service to authorized users. Information security includes those measures necessary to detect, document, and counter such threats. Information security is composed of computer security and communications security. Also called INFOSEC. (JP 1-02)

information system—The entire infrastructure, organization, personnel, and components that collect, process, store, transmit, display, disseminate, and act on information. (JP 1-02)

named area of interest—The geographic area where information that will satisfy a specific information requirement can be collected. Named areas of interest are usually selected to capture indications of adversary courses of action, but also may be related to conditions of the battlespace. Also called NAI. (JP 1-02)

request for information—**1.** Any specific time-sensitive ad hoc requirement for intelligence information or products to support an ongoing crisis or operation not necessarily related to standing requirements or scheduled intelligence production. A request for information can be initiated to respond to operational requirements and will be validated in accordance with the theater command's procedures. **2.** The National Security Agency/Central Security Service uses this term to state ad hoc signals intelligence requirements. Also called RFI. (JP 1-02)

situational awareness—Knowledge and understanding of the current situation which promotes timely, relevant, and accurate assessment of friendly, enemy, and other operations within the battlespace in order to facilitate decisionmaking. An informational perspective and skill that foster an ability to determine quickly the context and relevance of events that are unfolding. (MCRP 5-12C).

REFERENCES AND RELATED PUBLICATIONS

Joint Publications (JP)

0-2	Unified Action Armed Forces (UNAAF)
1-02	Department of Defense Dictionary of Military and Associated Terms
3-0	Doctrine for Joint Operations
6-0	Doctrine for C4 Systems Support to Joint Operations
6-02	Joint Doctrine for Employment of Operational/Tactical C4 Systems

Chairman of the Joint Chiefs of Staff (CJCSI)

3151.01	Global Command and Control System Common Operational Picture Reporting Requirements

Marine Corps Doctrinal Publications (MCDPs)

1	Warfighting
1-0	Marine Corps Operations (under development)
1-1	Strategy
1-2	Campaigning
1-3	Tactics
4	Logistics
5	Planning
6	Command and Control

Marine Corps Warfighting Publication (MCWP)

5-1	Marine Corps Planning Process

Marine Corps Reference Publications (MCRPs)

5-12C	Marine Corps Supplement to the Department of Defense Dictionary of Military and Associated Terms
6-23A	Multiservice Procedures for Joint Task Force—Information Management

Miscellaneous

Congress, House, *Federal Records Act*, chapter 21, "National Archives and Records Administration," and chapter 33, "Disposal of Records," U.S. Code Title 44, *Public Printing and Documents*